Invisible Students, Impossible Dreams:
experiencing vocational education 14-19

Invisible Students, Impossible Dreams:
experiencing vocational education 14-19

Liz Atkins

Trentham Books
Stoke on Trent, UK and Sterling, USA

Trentham Books Limited
Westview House   22883 Quicksilver Drive
734 London Road   Sterling
Oakhill   VA 20166-2012
Stoke on Trent   USA
Staffordshire
England ST4 5NP

First published 2009

British Library Cataloguing-in-Publication Data
A catalogue record for this book is available from the British Library

ISBN: 978 1 85856 451 7

An earlier version of chapter 2appeared in *Research in Post-compulsory Education*, vol 10, no 3, 2005. I am grateful to Routledge and Taylor for permission to re-publish.

Designed and typeset by Trentham Books Ltd and printed in Great Britain by Cpod Ltd, Trowbridge.

Contents

List of tables and graphics

Acronyms

AVCE	Advanced Vocational Certificate in Education
BTEC	Business and Technical Certificate
CACHE	Council for Awards in Children's Care and Education
CPVE	Certificate in Pre-Vocational Education
DES	Department of Education and Science
DFES	Department for Education and Skills
DIDA	Diploma in Digital Applications
E2E	Entry to Employment
EBD	Emotionally and Behaviourally Disturbed
EMA	Educational Maintenance Allowance
FE	Further Education
GCSE	General Certificate of Secondary Education
GNVQ	General National Vocational Qualification
HE	Higher Education
HND	Higher National Diploma
HSC	Health and Social Care
IT	Information Technology
LDD	Learning Difficulties and Disabilities
LEA	Local Education Authority
LSC	Learning and Skills Council
LSCN	Learning and Skills Council Nottinghamshire
MSC	Manpower Services Commission
NEET	Not in Employment, Education or Training
NQF	National Qualifications Framework
NVQ	National Vocational Qualifications
OCN	Open College Network
OFSTED	Office for Standards in Education
PCE	Post Compulsory Education
PCET	Post Compulsory Education and Training
PSE	Personal and Social Education
TVEI	Technical and Vocational Education Initiative
VET	Vocational Education and Training
VGCSE	Vocational General Certificate of Secondary Education
YOP	Youth Opportunities Programme
YTS	Youth Training Scheme

Acknowledgements

Firstly, my thanks are due to the anonymous students of Woodlands and St. Dunstan's Colleges for welcoming me into their lives and giving me so much help and information, and to the lecturers at both Colleges for being so generous with their interest, time and support.

The EdD thesis which forms the basis for this book would not have been completed without the enthusiasm, interest and critical friendship of my supervisor, Ann-Marie Bathmaker, now at the University of the West of England. She is an inspirational friend and teacher. My thanks are also due to Kathryn Ecclestone of Oxford Brookes who examined the thesis and gave much valuable feedback which has contributed to this book, and, I hope, improved it, and to Helen Colley of Manchester Metropolitan University, who has been a great source of encouragement. Thanks also to the many other friends and colleagues who have offered helpful commentaries and insights on different chapters of this book.

Thanks must also go to all the family and friends who have provided encouragement, but especially my husband, Ray Atkins, and my children, Tom, Bekah and Josh, whose tolerance and enduring support have sustained me throughout the genesis of this book, and my parents, 'scholarship children' of the 1940s whose commitment to the value of education and life experiences provided much of the motivation for this study. Finally, many, many thanks to Josh for drawing my attention to the quote by Matt Frei which heads Part 3 of this book, and to Hannah and Sean (owners of the feet) for the image on the front cover!

Part 1
14-19 vocational education:
history and context

We first crush people to the earth, and then claim the right of trampling on them forever, because they are prostrate (Lydia Maria Child, 1833)

Introduction

The 14-19 agenda, which has formed a key plank of Government education policy since its emergence in the 1999 White Paper *Learning to Succeed*, has been hotly debated both in the popular media and in academic circles. The debate essentially centres around different philosophical and political perspectives of education, both vocational and academic, the nature of vocational education and whether it can, or indeed should, be used to resolve perceived problems of low achievement and disaffection amongst teenagers. This book discusses the experiences of those who are the real focus of the 14-19 agenda – the low achieving or disaffected young people pursuing, at low levels, the broad vocational programmes which are currently being replaced by the Diploma. It draws conclusions about the relative value of a vocational education and considers the likely implications for the implementation of the Diploma.

My interest in this area relates both to my own experience as a vocational education student in the 1970s and to my later experience as a further education lecturer. During this time I worked mainly with students on level 1 and level 2 programmes. Individually, they had high aspirations and great pride in their achievements. One young woman, Kim, wept when she received the external notification of a pass in a GNVQ Foundation Unit. When I asked why she was crying, she replied 'no-one in our family's ever passed anything before'. Justifiably, she had great pride in her achievement and this was something I observed many times amongst these learners. Yet, dissonant with this, would be unexplained drop-outs, and the decisions of young people who aspired to technical and professional roles not to continue with their education beyond level 1 or level 2. It was also apparent that these young people presented challenges at a number of levels. Their behaviour in the classroom could be directly challenging, and many had difficulties in conforming to course and institutional requirements. They were problematised within the organisation and wider society as the 'disaffected' products of failing schools and, despite their individual expressions of motivation and high aspiration, many did not want to be in education but had little real choice in an economic climate which provided little in the way of work for unskilled 16 year olds, and in which state benefits were no longer available for unemployed 16-18 year olds.

At this time I worked at a Further Education (FE) college where few staff were keen to teach level 1or 2 students, preferring to concentrate on higher level learners who were perceived to be less demanding and to provide the lecturer with more satisfaction and greater recognition within the institutional academic hierarchy. Students on level 3 programmes tended to be disparaging about students on level 1 and 2 programmes. Together with wider societal perceptions, this seemed to suggest that within the hierarchy of low status vocational programmes in low status institutions a clear 'pecking order' existed and that level 1 students were right at the bottom and that the position for level 2 students was little better. This hierarchy is becoming ever more clearly defined as many FE colleges seek to develop Higher Education (HE) provision in response to funding imperatives and the widening participation, HE in FE agenda.

Effectively, the young people on programmes at levels 1 and 2 were perceived within the institution, and beyond it, to be less valuable learners, perhaps reflecting the 'sharp divide between valuable and non-valuable people and locales' described by Castells (2000:165). This situation led me to question how it felt to be a less valuable student, and in what ways it might be possible to demonstrate value for them. The research on which this book is based, and the participative approach to the fieldwork, reflect my attempt to answer those questions.

What this research tells us

Vocational education initiatives have been subject to significant amounts of research over the past 30 years (eg Bates *et al* in the 1980s; Hodkinson in the 1990s; and the more recent Transforming Learning Cultures (TLC) project). However, most of this is focused on A level equivalent credentials such as GNVQ Advanced, the parity of esteem debate and the extent to which vocational qualifications might be said to prepare young people for higher education. This is of little relevance to those undertaking lower level programmes who may not aspire to a Higher Education or who may not have the ability to achieve credentials at that level. There is little published research considering the needs and experiences of students undertaking vocational programmes at lower levels despite the facts that vocational education at these levels forms

4

the focus of the 14-19 agenda and that significant numbers of young people undertake lower level vocational programmes.

Thus, the level 1 foundation GNVQ has remained largely excluded from much of the official discourse about GNVQ (Bathmaker, 2001:86) and only three previous studies (Ainley and Bailey, 1997; Ball *et al*, 2000; Bathmaker, 2001) make specific reference to GNVQ foundation students; however, all these studies focused on a broader group and few foundation level students were involved in the research. Intermediate or level 2 programmes, whilst receiving more attention than the Foundation, have also been the subject of substantially less research than the Advanced qualification and similarly to the Foundation, much of the research which has been conducted investigated students undertaking a range of different levels of qualification (eg Abbott, 1997; Hodkinson, 1998 and Hodkinson and Bloomer, 2000). This is despite recent evidence to suggest that the curriculum currently available at level 1 is inadequate (Learning and Skills Council Nottinghamshire, 2005:22; Working Group on 14-19 Reform, 2003; 2004) and early criticisms of the standards on GNVQ Intermediate courses (Ofsted, 1993:26) which raised questions about the vocational curriculum at level 2.

When I was doing the fieldwork for this book, most young people undertaking vocational programmes, whether post-16 or as part of an alternative curriculum at 14-16, still pursued GNVQ programmes. The introduction of the GNVQ arose from the white paper *Education and Training for the 21st Century* (DES, 1991) and they were part of a strategy to increase participation and achievement in post-compulsory education and training (Bathmaker, 2001: 83). The Intermediate (level 2) and Advanced (level 3) levels were introduced in 1992, a year before the launch of the GNVQ Foundation (level 1). Such a massive initiative generated considerable interest from the academic community and consequently, most of the research into vocational education from that time focuses on GNVQ. They also became the vocational qualifications of choice for most colleges and for many of the schools which then offered a vocational alternative to GCSE.

Phased (if prolonged) withdrawal of the GNVQ began as a result of the Curriculum 2000 reforms, although some successor qualifications (eg AVCE) had very short lifespans. Future cohorts, both in school and colleges, will undertake the specialised Diploma which is currently being implemented as a part of the curriculum reforms arising from the 2005 White Paper (DfES, 2005). Mirroring the GNVQ in the scale of the initiative as well as the structure and content, its nomenclature is also similar, being available at Foundation (level 1), Higher (Level 2) and Advanced (Level 3).

Foundation GNVQ formed the lowest of the three levels of GNVQ awards and was positioned at the bottom end of the English National Qualifications Framework (NQF). Level 1 is equivalent to grades D-G at GCSE so is intended to meet the needs of those who have 'failed' at GCSE or, in the 14-16 phase, those who are not expected to achieve GCSE grades at A*-C. Although lower level credentials do appear on the framework, these are designed for students with learning difficulties and disabilities. Level 1 is the lowest point on the mainstream hierarchy but even so, the positioning of GNVQ foundation has been ambivalent in some institutions: Bathmaker (2001) found that it was regarded as mainstream in some institutions, and as special needs provision in others. This is significant given that most of the young people who enrol for such programmes have been educated in mainstream schools and entered for GCSE at 16+ or are pursuing an 'alternative' (but none-the-less main-stream) curriculum as part of the 14-19 reforms. Such positioning may be reflective of their position as a heavily problematised group, particularly in the context of vocational education which is largely perceived to be an appro-priate option for those who fall within a deficit model of 'disaffected', 'disad-vantaged' and 'low ability'.

The positioning of level 1 qualifications in particular, in a context of academic v. vocational qualifications, and at the bottom of a national hierarchy of credentials, suggests that they have low status and are of little value. This per-ception is reinforced when considered in the context of the skills agenda arising from the DfES publication *21st Century Skills: Realising Our Potential Individuals, Employers, Nation*, which states that level 2 qualifications are the 'minimum for employability' (2003b:13) a belief reinforced in a more recent white paper (DfES, 2006:4), and by the LSC (2007) who report data in terms of numbers achieving the 'Level 2 Attainment Threshold'. The positioning of level 2 in this way, as a 'minimum' credential also has negative connotations, diminishing the achievement, which may well be significant for the indivi-dual, and raises questions about the value of a vocational education at these levels.

The introduction of the Advanced GNVQ re-ignited the longstanding parity of esteem debate which was concerned with the fact that class divisions based on what was considered fit for people from different strata of society remain firmly entrenched within the education system (Woodward, 2002:3; McCulloch, 1994:60). These issues are reflected in the different value placed on academic and vocational curricula, and the social and class differences between those young people following an 'academic' route and those fol-lowing a 'vocational' route such as GNVQ or its successor qualifications.

Another factor which may have influenced the relative level of esteem for vocational qualifications is that they have traditionally been delivered in colleges of further education; often regarded as the Cinderella of the education system (Gleeson, 1996:84), a fact recognised in the Foster Review of further education which stated that 'FE colleges have a low profile on the national stage and a relatively poor image' (2005:5). In the context of 16-19 students, as Tomlinson (1997:10) has pointed out, post-16 education is a highly stratified and hierarchical system in which successful, high status institutions can choose high ability students, whilst others are forced to enrol the less desirable, unsuccessful learners who are 'firmly steered' towards vocational education.

The process which Tomlinson observed over a decade ago is now replicated in schools, as particular groups of 14 year olds are directed to the vocational programmes which are perceived to be easier than GCSE but which count as GCSE passes for the purpose of Government League tables. In this context of less successful learners undertaking vocational programmes, often in FE colleges, which are institutions with a poor image it is perhaps inevitable that the institutions, the learners and the vocational courses they undertake should come to be regarded as of low status.

Undertaking this research has provided an opportunity to explore these issues and to examine the ways in which they influence the aspirations and emerging learning identities of young people pursuing lower level vocational programmes. It has also facilitated a consideration of the nature of the opportunities offered by such programmes in an educational system which promotes lifelong learning as a means to economic success and emphasises the importance of increasingly higher levels of credential. Finally, it has provided an empirical basis from which to inform the debate about the dominant credentialist pedagogical model currently used in England, around which vocational programmes are constructed and which has been criticised as socially unjust (Lingard, 2005) and as judging 50 per cent of young people to have 'failed' halfway through the 14-19 phase (Working Group on 14-19 Reform, 2003:21).

Participative case study research

This research was conducted using a case study approach. As well as illuminating or generating understanding of something, case studies also reflect the values of the researcher. The personal values underpinning this research are strongly held and influenced all aspects of the research process, including the writing of this book, so it is important for me to outline them. I have a commitment to students stigmatised by perceived failure, and also a commitment to education, though a different model of education, as the means to address this. This commitment is rooted in my personal belief in the intrinsic value of each individual and it is on this belief that my commitment to the concept of social justice is founded. Inevitably, these values have been influenced by my life experiences: I have a stigmatised disability which was in part responsible for my impoverished early educational experiences and subsequent lack of achievement, and spent twelve years working as a psychiatric nurse amongst some of the most heavily stigmatised members of our society.

Informed by my values, I use a theoretical framework underpinned by a commitment to social justice in order to explore four over-arching questions:

- What does it mean to engage in vocational learning as a lower level student?
- How do lower level students construct their learning identities?
- What factors influence or constrain the development of those identities?
- What aspirations for the future do these students hold?

The book draws on a broad range of literature, and on empirical evidence from a study exploring the aspirations and learning identities of three groups of young people on vocational education programmes below level 3.

I would like to explain my reasons for choosing a case study approach, why I structured the research in the way that I did and also why I chose to present the data in narrative form. My reasons are related to the power of story-telling. Case study research provides the opportunity to examine and illuminate an issue or group in depth. Its use has been debated, and questions have been asked about whether it is possible to generalise the results of small scale studies such as this one. In this case, there is little other research, large scale or otherwise. However, where similar studies have been carried out, their findings have been broadly similar to those discussed here.

The great strength of case study is that it tells a story. The young people in this study certainly had a story to tell, and this also influenced my choice of a narrative presentation, which seemed to me to articulate more powerfully the reality of these young lives. This was important, as I was looking at abstract and subjective issues. Therefore, a case study approach allowed me to explore the issues which interested me within a framework in which it was possible to consider a broad range of issues that affected the young people. These included cultural, educational, economic and social factors such as class, gender, race and educational 'achievement'. Secondly, case study provided a framework in which a more inclusive research process could be developed, consistent with the social justice framework for the study.

This meant, for example, that the young people themselves contributed to the development of the questions which were used in the interviews and chose whether they wished to be interviewed individually or as part of a group. A multi-method approach using five different data gathering techniques was used. These were semi-structured interviews, conducted with both students and professionals, classroom observation, written data provided by the young people in the form of structured personal profiles and their responses to statements such as 'in five years time I would like to be...' plus some limited documentary evidence. I also made use of serendipitous data arising from the collaborative nature of the research process which was volunteered by students. This consisted of copies of the students' work, mainly in electronic form. The narratives in part 2 rely heavily on the interviews, and quote the young people verbatim in many places, but are also a synthesis of other data provided by the young people. This participative approach formed part of my attempt to demonstrate value and respect for the young people who were involved with the study and enable their voices to be heard as loudly as possible, to counter the way that lower level vocational students are perceived as less valuable than others.

Discourse and definitions

It has been argued that 'Language is not powerful in and of itself, but it becomes powerful when it is used in particular ways, or by particular groups and institutions' (Webb *et al*, 2002:95). This has particular relevance to lower level vocational students, who are 'othered' by forms of discourse which are overwhelmingly negative, including the use of terminology such as: disaffected, disadvantaged, disruptive or low achievers. The use of discourse of this nature is discussed later in this book, as is the nature of language such as: opportunities, qualifications, lifelong learning and employability, whose meaning, particularly in the context of government policy, is often contrary to the experience and lives of these students.

Other terms already used in the book also have their own, individual myriad meanings. For example, 'vocational' has been used in a variety of contexts over an extended period: what all definitions of the term share is that they bear some relationship to an occupation. Original definitions were the most specific, relating to 'a calling' and normally used in reference to occupations within the Church such as priests or those bound by monastic vows, and subsequently to occupations such as teaching and nursing. Later definitions widened the concept. Dewey (1916:307) referred to 'a direction of life activities as renders them perceptibly significant to a person because of the consequences they accomplish, and also useful to his associates', whilst the Oxford English Dictionary defines 'vocational' as 'a strong feeling of suitability for a particular career or occupation' (2003:1294).

In education, the term has been used more widely to refer to aspects of the curriculum that do not fall within the category of liberal or academic. Here I have defined vocational subjects as those which require some degree of applied knowledge and understanding and have a technical (applied) or occupational emphasis. The terms 'liberal' and 'academic' are used interchangeably, and refer to a traditional, theoretical curriculum including the core subjects of English, maths and science. The term 'parity of esteem' also has a long history. I use it to mean a position where vocational and academic qualifications receive equitable recognition and are divorced from existing associations and relationships with social class status.

Learning identities have been discussed at length elsewhere (eg Ball *et al*, 2000; Bathmaker, 2001). 'Learning identity' means that part of a young person's self which relates to their education, achievement and engagement with learning. This is discussed in terms of perceived and actual commitment to 'the course' and to learning, and in relation to other aspects of each young person's developing identity, such as gendered and social identities. 'Aspiration' is used to describe the young peoples career ambitions and their lifestyle ambitions. These are considered separately and are referred to as career aspirations and lifestyle aspirations.

The book also includes many references to 'engagement' and 'disengagement'. In policy terms, disengagement with learning usually refers to young people who are not achieving the outcomes expected of them (eg the 5 x A*-C benchmark at GCSE) whereas engagement with learning refers to achievement of targets or outcomes associated with credentials. However, teachers tend to use this term to describe a process of personal development and engagement with methods and activities, which they regard as more important. It is in this sense that the word is used here, except where it is framed in the context of government policy or discourse.

The term 'transition' is used to describe the once brief, now often extended period between completing compulsory education and entering the world of work. The young participants in the study are normally referred to as young people, but occasionally, mainly to avoid repetition, as students, since this also accurately describes them. The terms used to describe the groups of participants in part 2 reflect the descriptors used by the young people themselves as well as the programme they had enrolled on. Two groups were undertaking a GNVQ Foundation programme (level 1 within the National Qualifications Framework) and one group a locally designed pic'n'mix programme with multiple small accreditations referred to within the institution as 'level 1' but providing the opportunity to undertake some small credentials at level 2. Unless made explicit in the text, the term level 1 excludes National Vocational Qualifications (NVQs) at level 1, since they are occupational and work based and thus not considered in the context of this study, which relates specifically to full-time broad vocational provision.

The structure of the book

The book is structured in three broad sections, with the stories of the young people who took part in the research narrated between the policy and theoretical context in which they live their lives, and the theoretical analysis arising from them. This has the added advantage of allowing readers to make their own interpretations of the narratives. Part 1 discusses the theoretical and conceptual frameworks on which the empirical work was based, part 2 consists of the narratives of the participants and part 3 discusses the themes arising from the narratives and explores their implications for policy, research and practice in 14-19 education.

I have justified this study on the grounds of the paucity of existing empirical evidence relating to this group of young learners. I have declared my interest in this area locating my study within a value-based as well as an academic context and have raised a number of questions about the positioning and problematisation of 14-19 vocational students. The issues raised in this chapter are developed later in the book.

Chapter 1 considers the literature relevant to the study, moving from the historical and policy context of pre-vocational education to the development of GNVQ Foundation and Intermediate and their successor qualifications, exploring, as it does so, the relationship between vocational education and social inequality. Chapter 2 explores the positioning of 14-19 students on vocational programmes within a contemporary social and political context.

Chapter 3 provides a theoretical framework for the study, informed by contemporary academic literature in the field of social justice and by philosophic and religious texts. The chapter explores the concept of social justice with particular reference to inequalities in vocational education in England and in the context of a belief in the equal value of each individual. This concludes part one.

Part 2 of the book presents the data from the fieldwork in narrative form. Chapter 4 provides a context of the two institutions involved in the study, and an outline of the structure, content and curriculum of the programmes the students were pursuing. Chapter 5 presents the stories of the young people who were undertaking a GNVQ foundation award in Information Technology. Chapter 6 explores the stories of a group of young women enrolled on a similar programme in Health and Social Care, and chapter 7, the concluding chapter in part 2, represents the stories of a group of young people enrolled on a generic level 1/2 programme.

Part 3 discusses the 'little stories' (Griffiths, 2003:81) of the earlier narratives, with chapters 8 to 11 devoted to the key themes arising from the study. These chapters explore the dichotomy between the young people's stories and the reality of their present lives and likely futures as they attempt to use their agency to negotiate transitions and develop identities within the context of oppressive systemic and embodied structures. Finally, chapters 12 and 13 seek to draw clear conclusions from the study and to make recommendations for structural and pedagogical changes which could provide a more equitable and socially just context for the education of vocational learners in a 14-19 context

Summary

This book explores the aspirations and learning identities of three groups of young students who were enrolled on lower level vocational education programmes. Two of these groups were undertaking General National Vocational Qualification (GNVQ) foundation awards, and one a locally designed level 1/2 course. At the time the fieldwork for this book was undertaken, the GNVQ foundation was the only full time level 1 credential which was available nationally. It could be taken in eight vocational subjects but was due to be withdrawn from 2006 and replaced with BTEC successor credentials. Some organisations, including one of those involved in this study, had already rejected the GNVQ foundation in favour of locally designed programmes accredited through the Open College Network (OCN). Subsequent Government reforms, specifically the 2005 White Paper, have resulted in the implementation of the Specialised Diploma, which, whilst intended to complement the 14-19, rather than the traditional 16-19 curriculum, has many parallels with ancestor qualifications such as GNVQ.

1
History, policy and practice
in the 14-19 sector

Introduction

This chapter considers the historical and contemporary policy context in relation to vocational students, discussing how concerns about social inequality and parity of esteem led to the new vocationalism of the 1980s, specifically the pre-vocational programmes such as the Certificate in Pre-Vocational Education (CPVE) and the Technical and Vocational Education Initiative (TVEI) and then to programmes such as GNVQ and, more recently, the specialised Diploma. It illustrates how successive policy initiatives have failed to address fundamental issues of equity within what Tomlinson (1997: 1/17) described as a 'divided and divisive' system of post-16 education, and argues that contemporary 14-19 initiatives are also unlikely to do so.

Historical context

It has been suggested that the present educational system in this country offers tri-partite pathways arising from the Dearing *Review of Qualifications for 16-19 year olds* (1996). Following this, a range of government policies were published (eg DfES, 2002; DfES, 2003a), with the stated aim of redressing the issue of parity of esteem and of improving vocational education and raising its status in order to meet the economic demands created by changing employment patterns. Despite these intentions, the outcomes of both the 1991 White Paper (DES, 1991), and the Dearing Report (1996) were in fact a reinforcement of the *status quo* in terms of Advanced (level 3) qualifications, and failed to address the issues surrounding intermediate (level 2) and foundation (level 1) credentials. These papers formalised the triple-track qualifications system which offered the academic 'gold standard' A Levels, the

GNVQ and newly established NVQ as routes into training and employment. This system remains largely unchanged today. The names, though not the structure or content,of the vocational credentials are different, and the pathways now exist within a 14-19, rather than a 16-19, phase. However, the impact of pursuing one or other of the pathways in terms of life and economic chances will be the same for the young people who make 14+ options in 2009 and beyond as it was for those who made post-16 choices in the 1990s.

McCulloch (1995:128) has described this system as the 'new tripartite' and it may indeed be seen to echo the ancient Platonic concept of gold, silver and copper (Lee, 1955) as the employment, salary and thus the life opportunities offered by the different routes are widely different. Tomlinson (1997:4) speculated that this triple track was considered acceptable as it accords with the 40/30/30 society envisaged by Galbraith (1992) and Hutton (1995). She went on to argue that

> The three-track system currently becoming embedded is leading to a situation where young people are not educated to be equal citizens in the society or even members of the same economy. (*Ibid*:17)

If particular influences are channelling young people into routes which are perceived to be appropriate to their anticipated role in life, particularly if those routes are regarded as of lower value or offer less in the way of later opportunities, this would represent a clear re-inforcement of tripartism in English education and increase the levels of disadvantage already experienced by young people on low level vocational courses.

This issue is one of increasing importance within a social and economic context which places a clear focus on the high skills economy (DfES, 2003b) and a concomitant high value on learning and credentials. It is reflected in both the recent media reports of the government's intention to raise the school leaving age to 18 (BBC, 2006; Seager, 2009) and in the ongoing expectation that all citizens will engage in lifelong learning.

The English tradition of education has its roots in the influential and successful public schools of the nineteenth century, which emphasised, amongst other things, the value of the classical, liberal curriculum. This curriculum, with its study of classical literature and languages, was deeply rooted in the Platonic concept of education for leadership (McCulloch, 1991:10/11) and became institutionalised within the state education system through the 1868 Public Schools Act and later, the 1902 Education Act which established mass secondary education.

It was the Norwood report (1943), however, that was used as the basis for the 1944 Education Act, and this established a tripartite system based on the Platonic ideal which was founded on the premise that Grammar, Technical and Modern schools would be established in each borough. These would provide different types of education, ostensibly related to the needs and abilities of each child. However, in the post-war struggle to reconstruct, few technical schools were ever opened, resulting in the mass of children receiving a secondary modern education and a minority receiving a grammar school education. This system created clear structural inequalities which reinforced class and social differences, largely denying educational opportunity to children from the lower social classes (McCulloch, 1998:1).

The liberal curriculum was necessary to gain entry to higher education and the professions. A levels, introduced in 1957, became the passport' for this to happen. The differences within the education system reflected and re-inforced the differing values placed on occupational roles within society. Within this context, it was perhaps inevitable that the liberal 'academic' curriculum, providing as it did a passport to university and the professions, should come to be regarded as superior to the vocational curriculum which was followed in the modern and technical schools, and led to at best a craft apprenticeship but to unskilled, low status employment for all too many young people.

The type of school they attended and consequently the type of curriculum they had access to divided children and reinforced the class divisions between the affluent middle classes who were in a position to access the liberal curriculum offered by the Grammar schools, and the working classes who were not. The tensions between the vocational and academic curriculum and their relationship to class was noted as early as 1868 by the Taunton Commission and in the early 20th Century Whitehead (1929:74) argued that 'the antithesis between a technical and a liberal education is fallacious'. Many government initiatives since have sought to foster parity of esteem between different types of qualification (eg Board of Education, 1938; DES, 1991; DfES, 2003a, 2005). However, the comment in the 2005 white paper that 'Vocational education and training for young people have low credibility and status in this country' (DfES, 2005:17) suggests that each new initiative has multiple echoes of a failed past. None of these earlier initiatives has succeeded in addressing the fundamental issue of social inequality and so most vocational programmes are still taken by the *less* equal, something which is indivisible from the parity of esteem debate.

New vocationalism

Progressive educational reforms, ostensibly intended to tackle inequality, were pursued from the 1970s to the early 1980s and were increasingly criticised as being forms of 'new vocationalism' (eg Cohen, 1984; Finn, 1984; 1985; Dale, 1985). The term evolved within a context of mass youth unemployment as educational researchers began to distinguish between traditional vocational job *preparation* and new initiatives aimed at achieving job *readiness*. These initiatives came to be criticised as being 'narrow and divisive' (McCulloch, 1987:32) forms of preparation for unemployment, rather than preparation for meaningful work (Bates *et al*, 1984) and included programmes such as the Youth Opportunities Programme (YOP) Youth Training Scheme (YTS), Technical and Vocational Education Initiative (TVEI), and the Certificate in Pre-Vocational Education (CPVE). Despite criticism from the academic community, government rhetoric was much more positive.

Sikes and Taylor (1987:60) highlighted conflicting views of the TVEI initiative, these being the official government discourse promoting it as a 'liberating reform' and a more critical perception which viewed the initiative as 'an invidious attempt to re-introduce the iniquities of occupational and even socio-cultural segregation'. David Young, the principal architect of the TVEI initiative, regarded it as the major part of the answer to youth unemployment (Pring, 1995:63) and defended it as a technical curriculum for young people who liked 'doing as well as learning' (Edwards, 1997:19), perhaps inadvertently reinforcing artificial divisions between the liberal and vocational curricula. Weston *et al* (1995 cited in Brooks, 1998:14) suggested that for 'low attainers' the TVEI initiative had a positive impact in terms of attitudes towards and participation in, post 16 education. Such comments arguably reinforce divisions between vocational and academic education, in terms of both the implication that different types of young people are suited to different types of education and in the context of the negative discourse used to describe those undertaking vocational programmes, thus generating a deficit model for the 'low- attaining' young people 'suited' to vocational education.

The impetus for the original initiatives may be traced back to the social and economic imperatives highlighted in Callaghan's Ruskin Speech of 1976. This landmark speech not only marks the date at which the 'New Vocationalism' policies originated, but also when economic policy first became the driver for education policy. Millman and Weiner (1987:167) argued that the introduction of new vocationalist initiatives was premised on the belief that schools and education were partly responsible for the failure of so many young people to find employment. Tellingly, TVEI was created by the Department for

Industry, rather than the Department of Education and Science (DES) and control over education and training became centralised as the Manpower Services Commission (MSC) exerted considerable influence over the colleges via YTS and over schools via TVEI (Gleeson, 1987:4). Such centralised control continued beyond the demise of the MSC to the national curriculum for schools and the influence of the Learning and Skills Council (LSC) over the curriculum offer in colleges and other post-16 providers. Whilst none of the early initiatives survives in its original form, many subsequent initiatives had their origins in the new vocationalism of the 1980s and 1990s. These include General National Vocational Qualifications, Business and Technical Certificate qualifications, National Vocational Qualifications, vocational GCSEs (VGCSEs) and the specialised Diplomas introduced in September 2008.

The Diploma, particularly at levels 1 and 2, may be regarded as a successor to the pre-vocational initiatives of TVEI and CPVE. In 1985, Brockington, White and Pring (1985:35) outlined the proposals for the CPVE. The programme was to have a common core, use experiential learning methods and have a vocationally relevant, skills based curriculum. The aim of the programme was to equip young people with the basic skills, knowledge and attitudes they would need in adult life. Writing in 1989, Gleeson found these to be common features with the BTEC foundation and TVEI programmes. Similarly, the specialised Diploma which mirrors the GNVQ in both structure and content has, at levels 1 and 2 at least, more in common with its pre-vocational predecessors than with the increasingly 'academicalised' Level 3 vocational programmes such as BTEC National awards. These higher level awards have followed an increasingly academic route, particularly since the advent of curriculum 2000, in an attempt to achieve and demonstrate parity with the A level curriculum. However, the parity of esteem debate is of little relevance for programmes which lie at the bottom of an educational hierarchy at a point where no 'academic' alternative is available. What matters here is the nature of the curriculum, the type of work it is preparing young people for, and the relationship between the programme and social class. Lower level vocational programmes follow a narrow, occupationally based curriculum which socialises young people to certain types of occupation and reinforces existing social class divisions.

Contemporary broad vocational programmes (such as BTEC Introductory and First Certificates and Diplomas including the new Diplomas and occupational programmes such as NVQ) cover a limited range of information and are assessed against standardised and nationally approved criteria. Content tends to emphasise what Unwin described nearly two decades ago as 'routine and practical' (1990:196), as well as skills such as adaptability and reliability, perceived to enable young people to 'buy in' to, and become successful in, a new, post-Fordist workplace order (Usher and Edwards, 1994:106; Helsby *et al*, 1998:63; Bathmaker, 2001:85). Further, the contemporary vocational curriculum is offered predominantly within the FE sector and has been argued to be class specific and accessed largely by young people from lower socio economic groups (Colley *et al*, 2003:479; Macrae *et al*, 1997:92) despite evidence that students are very much aware that the choices made within the three track system carry 'different messages about desirability and exchange value within the labour market' (Tomlinson, 1997:10).

The aims of the new vocational programmes, have also been criticised for preparing young people for a particular role in the workplace. Clarke and Willis (1984:3) argued that the perception that young people need to be inculcated with not only the skills but also the right *attitudes* for work had its orgins in Callaghan's Great Debate of 1976 and noted how this perception was justified in the context of the mass youth unemployment of the time. Moore (1984:66) went further, arguing that that there was an associated view that the young people who required inculcation with the right attitudes and skills for work belonged to a particular category of non-academic low achievers, thus assuming a deficit model for these young people. Programmes such as CPVE and latterly GNVQ inculcated social disciplines such as team-work, attendance and punctuality (Cohen, 1984:105; Chitty, 1991b:104) and thus preparing young people for specific, low pay, low skill occupations (Ainley, 1991:103; Helsby *et al*, 1998:74; Bathmaker, 2001). This pre-ordained positioning within the labour market therefore becomes a determinant of future life chances and contributes to the replication of social class in future generations.

Policy failings

The White Paper *14-19 Opportunity and Excellence* (DfES, 2003a) proposed significant changes, including the expansion of vocationally orientated GCSEs and the introduction of a statutory 'work and enterprise' component to the 14-19 curriculum. However, anecdotal evidence suggests that uptake of vocational GCSEs was highest amongst low-achieving and 'disengaged' young people. Attempting to re-engage young people with education through work-related learning may have some value but can produce some unfortunate effects. The short-lived VGCEs, like other recent vocational credentials, were perceived as lacking in rigour and being suitable only for those who are less valued as learners – the low achievers and the disaffected. Furthermore, the lack of parity of esteem between the 'academic' and the vocational subjects in the curriculum is re-inforced. Ofsted (2003:5) recognised this and suggested that parity is more likely to be achieved where significant numbers of young people across the ability range are engaged in vocational learning rather than only those who are disaffected or have academic difficulties.

It has also been argued that there is evidence of resistance to new qualifications within schools, particularly those qualifications that have a vocational emphasis (Holland *et al*, 2003:5). More recently, concerns about the Diploma, launched in September 2008, were reflected in a take-up of 12,000 nationally, in comparison to the 50,000 predicted by Government (Woolcock, 2008). Whilst such entrenched attitudes towards vocational education are apparent, the likely consequence is that lower level vocational programmes will continue to be perceived as suitable for those problematised within a deficit model as low ability, disengaged and disaffected and that such young people will be perceived as suitable only for low level vocational programmes, effectively extending the deficit model to include the educational programme as well as the young person undertaking it.

Parallel with the implementation of the 2003 White Paper (DfES, 2003a) were the deliberations of the Working Group on 14-19 Reform, chaired by Mike Tomlinson. In 2002, following widespread concern about examination standards arising from discrepancies in A level marking, the debate about qualifications broadened and came to involve the more popular sections of the media, rather than being confined to the academic press. This led to pressure on government and, eventually, the resignation of the education secretary, Estelle Morris, and the dismissal of the head of QCA. Part of the Government response to this was the establishment of the Working Group whose remit was to 'develop proposals for major reform of the curriculum and qualifications in England for young people aged approximately 14-19' (Working Group on 14-19 Reform, 2003:01)

The final report, published in 2004, endorsed a baccalaureate system broadly similar to that proposed by Hodgson and Spours (2003). The Committee's proposals suggested creating a qualifications system from entry level to level three within an overarching Diploma. Whilst this was designed to facilitate movement between different tracks or pathways, it was criticised both for retaining a broad triple-track approach which encompassed academic, vocational and occupational study and for proposing the abolition of A level and GCSE credentials. Much of this criticism again appeared in the popular media and, despite widespread support in the education sector, the proposals were rejected by a Labour government which was facing a third general election.

Instead, the government responded with a much watered down version in the 2005 White Paper *14-19 Education and Skills*, which retained A levels and GCSEs and was consequently more acceptable to voters.

Whilst it may have been acceptable to voters, the impact of the policy on young people who struggle to achieve at level 2 or above may not be entirely positive. The 2005 paper remains at the implementation stage and although it identifies the intention to remove the expectation of achievement of level 2 at 16 (DfES, 2005:46) this remains acknowledged as a minimum level of achievement with entry and level 1 qualifications described as 'steps on the way' (DfES, 2005:6). Moreover, achievement data published by the LSC identify level 2 as the 'minimum attainment threshold' also suggesting that it is the most basic form of credential. This approach is hardly motivating to those young people for whom level 2 represents a significant achievement. It also fails to acknowledge or address a number of other issues. Level 1 credentials are likely to remain lacking in value where there is a clear expectation that level 2 is a baseline level of achievement and young people who have achieved qualifications at levels 1 and 2 will be perceived to lack value in an economic context which values ever higher levels of credential.

The notion of failure will not go away for these young people and the difficulties associated with an extended transition are not addressed, particularly for young people in difficult circumstances. It seems likely that many young people, rather than continuing in what they may regard as a fruitless attempt to gain ever higher levels of credential, will leave education and either enter low pay, low skill employment or become part of the Not in Employment, Education or Training (NEET) population. Initiatives such as personalised learning (DfES, 2006) are also likely to impact significantly on this group of young people though it seems unlikely that any of them will adequately address the fundamental issues of social inequality in the English education system.

Finally, and perhaps most worryingly, the Diploma framework fails to acknowledge the very significant differences between those young people who are able to achieve the baseline level 2 at 16+ and those who will be 18+ before achieving this level of credential. Concerns about the policy direction of 14-19 education and the 'unprecedented amount of policy initiatives' were raised in the 2006 report of the Nuffield Review (Hayward *et al*, 2006:4) which also argued that 'partial reforms, together with the weaknesses of organisational arrangements, may be unable to address pressing issues of social division and inefficiencies in 14-19 provision'. It may be argued that such social divisions and inefficiencies disproportionately affect and disadvantage those young people who currently undertake vocational education programmes and that, despite a plethora of government policies in recent years including the introduction of the Diploma, this issue is coming back to haunt us even more.

The Specialised Diplomas are intended by Government to provide a vocational route from 14-19, but there are a number of significant problems in their design and purpose. In a field which already makes wide (and diverse) use of the term Diploma as the nomenclature for qualifications ranging from level 2 to post-graduate, the introduction of a suite of new qualifications, all called Diploma and at 3 different levels, is confusing to many. More importantly, and as noted by Hodgson and Spours (2007) there are tensions and conflicts in the purpose and design of these new credentials. They are intended to meet the very different needs of young people in compulsory education and those in post-compulsory education across the 14-19 age range.

This means that they are intended to be equally suitable for a high achieving young person hoping to enter Higher Education as for a young person who is disaffected with education by the age of 14 or one who, having gained D-G grade GCSEs, will struggle to achieve a level 2 by 18+. Where a young person is 18 before achieving level 2, but wishes to progress to level 3, the narrow vocational specialisms effectively create a repetitious spiral curriculum, which will last for four years.

In some sectors, implementation 14-16 will be difficult. In Health and Social Care, a popular subject implemented in 2008 for example, entry to employment is restricted to those aged 18+ and occupational (NVQ) level 2 qualifications are the minimum acceptable to work in the field. This would make a level 2 Diploma in those subjects unsuitable for a young person hoping to enter employment or an apprenticeship at 16 and will create issues with placement experience. Many care organisations will not wish to accept a young person on placement into an environment which is subject to very significant legal requirements and restrictions, including CRB clearance for all working there.

At a broader level, the Nuffield Review of 14-19 Education (2007) has suggested that the new Diplomas are located as a 'middle track' within the 14-19 curriculum, something which they point out has failed in the past. The paper concludes that the Diplomas can only succeed if they are introduced as part of a single, comprehensive Diploma framework as recommended by the Working Group on 14-19 Reform (2004). Allen (2007:299) considers that

Diplomas exhibit many of the weaknesses and contradictions of existing vocational qualifications, and are thus likely to perpetuate existing divisions between the academic and vocational curriculum. Hodgson and Spours (2007:657) argue that far from transforming 14-19 education, the failure to reform academic qualifications alongside their vocational equivalents

> is likely to result in 'academic drift', lack of status and a relatively low level of uptake for these new awards, a process compounded by low employer recognition of broad vocational qualifications.

These concerns suggest that, far from providing solutions to perceived problems in 14-19 education, the current initiative is more likely to re-inforce existing social class and educational inequities and inequalities.

Summary

This chapter has reviewed the historical and political context surrounding the development of vocational education in an attempt to contextualise the current position of vocational education in the 14-19 phase. It has found that there are obvious inequalities between those following academic and those following vocational routes 14-19 and that, despite a multiplicity of government initiatives ostensibly designed to address them, each of these initiatives has failed. Consequently, the social and moral challenges posed by social and educational divisions remain and seem unlikely to be resolved by current initiatives such as the implementation of specialised Diplomas. It seems almost inconceivable that such issues should persist in the 21st Century, and more than 140 years after the Taunton Commission (1868) first noted the relationship between social class and vocational and liberal education.

2

The invisible cohort: lower level vocational students

Introduction

Chapter 1 considered the historical and contemporary policy context in relation to vocational education and the 14-19 agenda. Chapter 2 explores what it means to be a 14-19 student on a vocational programme at the beginning of the 21st Century within a social and educational context which emphasises the importance and value of engaging with life-long learning. The chapter focuses on those young people who do not achieve the minimum level 2 at 16, but who may achieve that level of credential by 18+. This includes young people working in the new Diploma framework who achieve level 1 at 16 and those taking GCSEs whose results profile is below 5 A*-C grades and who subsequently progress to post-16 vocational education at level 1 or 2. It explores how the students on such programmes are viewed by the institutions at which they study, policy makers and wider society, suggesting that they are perceived as being of potentially low economic value, and consequently low social value. It considers the likely consequences for young people of undertaking a low level, low value vocational programme and, drawing on contemporary literature, suggests that these are likely to involve a lifetime of casualised, low pay, low skill drudgery.

Excluded from debate

As discussed in chapter 1, post compulsory education in England has undergone major upheavals over the past 30 years, and increasingly vocal demands have been made for the development of a system which offers both parity of esteem across academic and vocational qualifications and equality of opportunity to all learners. This rhetoric has co-existed with a policy context which has become increasingly driven by economic imperatives.

Debates around parity of esteem have tended to focus on the divide between A levels and their vocational equivalents at level 3, and education policy has increasingly emphasised the perceived need to increase the skill and educational levels of workers (DfES, 2002; DfES, 2003a; DfES, 2003b). Together, these phenomena have served to create a situation where the focus of policy and debate has been confined to those learners functioning at level 2 (GCSE equivalent) and above, although significant investment in basic skills in recent years has begun to address some of the needs of more mature learners functioning at lower educational levels and who have few or no academic credentials. Largely excluded from such policy and debate have been those young people working at or towards level 1 during their transition across KS4 and beyond and into work, only some of whom may achieve level 2 credentials by 18+.

Level 1 qualifications such as the BTEC Introductory Certificate and Diploma, and the newly launched specialised Diplomas, may be found towards the bottom end of the National Qualifications Framework (NQF). The NQF recognises English and Welsh credentials within a framework which allocates, in principle at least, notional equivalence between qualifications from Entry to Doctoral level. Level 1 is defined within the framework as the ability to 'employ a narrow range of applied knowledge and basic comprehension' (QCA), and is offered largely within Colleges of Further Education during the post-compulsory phase of education and, increasingly, in schools and colleges as part of the 14-19 agenda. Level 2 learning is described by QCA as the ability to 'apply knowledge with underpinning comprehension in a number of areas' and encompasses vocational qualifications such as those listed above as well as the benchmark 5 A*-C GCSE grades.

In 2002 the Green Paper *14-19 Extending Opportunities, Raising Standards* (DfES, 2002:12) referred to the need to 'promote parity of esteem between vocational and academic programmes of study' as part of its proposal to reform the 14-19 phase and introduce what was then termed a 'matriculation diploma'. Since then, the phrase has largely disappeared from policy documents, to be replaced by commitments to 'a much stronger vocational offer' (DfES, 2003a:13), increased work based learning in schools, the development of the Modern Apprenticeship system, the introduction of vocational programmes with 'occupational relevance' and the development of the Foundation Degree (DfES, 2003b). Despite this plethora of initiatives, the 2005 White Paper still recognises that vocational education and training have low status and little credibility in England (DfES, 2005:17).

Within this poorly regarded vocational system, students working towards level 2 remain invisible, victims of a lack of esteem and significant structural barriers at a number of different levels. These include the lack of choice and opportunity arising from the limited range of vocational programmes available at level 1 (Working Group on 14-19 Reform, 2004a:17). The only alternative to the vocational programmes available would be to spend a further two years on GSCE programmes – repeating an experience at which the young person is already perceived to have 'failed'. Other barriers include the ambivalent positioning of level 1 programmes, sometimes located as a mainstream programme, and sometimes as special needs provision, and the fact that whatever their achievement at level 1, the reality as most young people and their tutors see it is that only advanced programmes have any currency outside the institution (Bathmaker, 2002). Further, there is the commitment required to a very extended progression – to achieve a Higher Education credential a student achieving a level 1 Diploma at 16+ would have to 'progress' through three or four years of Further Education, and a further two years of Higher Education to achieve a Foundation Degree or three to four years to achieve a Bachelors degree.

Despite these issues around level 1 vocational learning, and the wealth of research into Advanced level GNVQ, the foundation programme received little critical examination. One possible reason for this may be the relatively small numbers of young people to have been registered for the award during its lifetime (Raggatt and Williams, 1999:16) together with the traditionally low achievement rates associated with GNVQ qualifications. In 2002 the Government consulted on the withdrawal of the 6 unit (levels 1 and 2) GNVQs. The same year, success rates on foundation GNVQ programmes stood at 83 per cent. However, this figure refers to completers, and effectively discounts the young people who withdraw during the programme. When the figures are adjusted to reflect this, the success rate for 2001/2002 was only 62 per cent in the context of a national retention rate of 77 per cent (LSC, 2002).

These significant levels of non-achievement, both in terms of failure to complete the programme or to achieve on completion, are reflected in research carried out by Ball *et al* (2000) in their study of a cohort of young people from a North London Comprehensive, as well as by Bathmaker (2001). Bathmaker interviewed seven foundation students towards the end of their programme, and found that they reported largely positive experiences. However, these were the young people who had, perhaps for the first time in their lives, experienced success and this may have been an influencing factor in their perceptions of the programme. Those who had withdrawn may have had a different perspective.

In a longitudinal study Ball *et al* identified nine students from a total of 59 (15%) who entered foundation GNVQ programmes, and a further two who entered NVQ level one programmes. Two years later, two of those who entered GNVQ could not be contacted, and of the remaining seven the outcomes for four were discussed. One had become a mother, one had progressed through Intermediate to GNVQ Advanced, one was unemployed and one was considering doing A levels and entering Higher Education in Australia. All were defined as having factors in their lives which might lead to social, educational and/or economic exclusion. Whilst this research is based on very small samples, it consistently suggests that very few young people entering the post compulsory sector at level 1 will fulfil the policy rhetoric about individual responsibility, lifelong learning and opportunities for all and progress through the system to level 3 or beyond.

Data from the same study identified eight young people on level 2 programmes in 1996. One of these was re-taking GCSEs and seven were enrolled on GNVQ Intermediate programmes. Three years later, two had progressed to HE, the outcome for one, a refugee, was unknown, and four were in employment. Similarly to the level 1 students, all experienced exclusionary characteristics. Whilst their outcomes might be regarded as comparatively better than those of the level 1 students, they illustrate starkly the difficulties associated with an extended transition and the very small numbers who fulfil the rhetoric of opportunity and progression and an eventual transition to high pay, high skill employment.

Despite using policy rhetoric which conflates progression with straightforward transitions, DfES have recently acknowledged that not all qualifications offered progression routes to higher levels (DfES, 2005:19) and the Nuffield Review (2006) has identified a lack of clarity in some vocational pathways from level 3 to Higher Education. Together with the limited range of options at level 1 (Working Group on 14-19 Reform, 2003, 2004a, 2004b), this suggests that the articulation of progression pathways is poor in many areas across all levels of vocational education, creating additional structural barriers which are absent for those young people following a more traditional transition from GCSE to A level and subsequently Higher Education. More recently Colley *et al* (2008) have argued that the introduction of Diplomas means that young peoples' choices are not only posed at an earlier age but are 'less certain in terms of progression, both vertically and horizontally'.

Excluded by policy

The reality of the lives of these young people reflects an English education policy which, over the past 20 years, has resulted in an increasingly credentialist and divisive system of secondary and tertiary education. According to government policy rhetoric, the emphasis on higher level skills (and thus qualifications) will mean that '...we will develop an inclusive society that promotes employability for all' (DfES, 2003b:18). Employability in this context is defined by the holding of level 2 credentials, but the still higher value placed on level 3 and Higher Education credentials is also evident in current policy documents as well as in the targets arising from them, such as 90 per cent of 22 year olds to achieve minimum level 3 by 2010, together with 50 per cent participation in Higher Education by 2010 (DfES, 2003a; DfES, 2003b). The Skills Strategy (DfES, 2003b) makes no specific mention of level one qualifications, other than in terms of individuals who do not hold level 2.

This increasingly skills-driven agenda places a clear value (whether high or low) on individuals according to their perceived economic potential, which rises with each level of educational attainment. Added to this, a different value is placed on academic credentials such as GCSE and A level which also provide clearer educational progression routes and, beyond these, better occupational prospects. This leads to a situation where young people who pursue a vocational route 14-19, where level 2 is not achieved until the age of 19, are effectively working towards qualifications which have at best (level 2) minimal, and at worst (level 1) no economic value but which position them where they can only progress to low pay, low skill work or exchange their credentials for more cultural capital, but only in the form of vocational qualifications in relatively low status institutions (Colley, 2006:25).

The lack of value placed on level 1 qualifications in particular is also evident in outcomes at 16, where young people achieving five good GCSEs (defined as grades A*-C) have attained level 2. However, those young people achieving at grades D-G, even where the grade achieved represents significant personal achievement, have attained level one by default – that is by failing to achieve level two. The attribution of failure to almost half the young people who take GCSE examinations each year was recognised by the Working Group on 14-19 Reform (2004a:17), who proposed a new post-14 structure which clearly identified a need for recognition of achievement at all levels as part of a broader inclusiveness agenda. However, it could be argued that the inclusiveness agenda subscribed to by the 14-19 Working Group also acted to reinforce the concept of level 1 students as a problematised group by acknowledging level 2 achievement as being consistent with the concept of employability and the ability to contribute to society.

The Working Group proposed a new qualifications structure which was intended to address these difficulties, but inherent within that structure was the assumption that the student would be capable of progressing, would wish to progress through the levels proposed and would have the necessary economic, social and emotional support to do so, an assumption or expectation also found in current policy documents (DfES, 2003a:17; 2003b:127, 2005:6). The Group also recognised the need to improve the curriculum at lower levels, having identified '...an absence of consistently high quality level one programmes and qualifications' (Working Group on 14-19 Reform, 2004:17), an added barrier to any young person wishing to progress to a level 1 option post-16.

Despite the limited range of level 1 qualifications, the Green Paper *14-19 Extending Opportunities, Raising Standards* (2002) proposed that all 6 unit GNVQ qualifications should be withdrawn and replaced by applied GCSEs (previously Vocational GCSEs or VGCSEs), with a level 1 qualification being equivalent to D-G grade. Whilst students who took Foundation GNVQ programmes and those pursuing its successor qualifications may be subject to the types of inequity outlined above, which will constrain all aspects of their future life, such qualifications have two significant advantages over the GCSE. Firstly, they are perceived as easier to achieve and to offer a route to intermediate qualifications by the students (Bathmaker, 2001; Ball *et al*, 2000), and secondly they offer a level 1 credential by achievement rather than failure, a significant factor in terms of young people's self confidence, as well as their motivation to continue in education. Representations from Post-Compulsory Education and Training (PCET) professionals resulted in a policy compromise on this issue, and the White Paper decreed that both 6 unit GNVQ and Applied GCSE should continue to operate until 'suitable alternatives' (to GNVQ) were available. (DfES, 2003a:25)

Awarding Bodies filled the gap left by Foundation GNVQ with the introduction of BTEC level 1 awards to complement the long standing Level 2 First Diploma and, despite the introduction of the specialised Diploma, these will continue to be the main option (or opportunity) for those young people who do not achieve a minimum level 2 by 16+, and for whom broad vocational qualification is the only option.

So whilst the rhetoric of current post-16 education policy espouses 'opportunity for all', this in fact conflicts with many of the outcomes of that policy. For young people working towards level 2 post-16, the outcomes are largely negative, and in no way reflect the emphasis on opportunity. These young people are consigned to the lowest level vocational programmes, which have little social, educational or economic recognition. Significant structural, social and economic barriers stand in the way of further educational progression. Associated with the low esteem placed on the occupations and life opportunities they may be able to access, this can only result in the creation of a cohort of young people who are perceived as non-valuable by government, wider society, and themselves.

Tomlinson links these divisive policies with the continued reproduction of a class structure which results in the exclusion of those who do not have access to a good education, reflected in the type of credentials they achieve, and which allows more privileged social groups to 'maximise reproduction of their own advantages' (2001:261). Indeed, Castells (2000:165/167) argues that such divisions result in the 'territorial confinement of systematically worthless populations, disconnected from networks of valuable functions and people' a 'fourth world' of the socially excluded who, he argues, are found in both the developed and the developing worlds. Corbett (1997:174) notes that the conflation of 'good citizenship' with a job, a home and social skills 'effectively dismisses a whole section of young people who have left school underqualified' and Coffield (1999:484) argues that the different value placed on different levels of credential creates an 'educational apartheid'.

In relation to the young people discussed here, such a situation can only be compounded by the lack of critical examination of the needs of lower level vocational learners, particularly in the post-16 phase, which renders them invisible to academics and policy makers. This absence of critical examination means that much of the policy which impacts heavily on them is based on perceived wisdom or assumption rather than current, credible research or the 'policy memory' advocated by Higham and Yeomans (2006).

Education or socialisation to casual employment?

Raggatt and Williams (1999:142) have suggested that the re-naming of the GNVQ awards in 1993 as Foundation, Intermediate and Advanced was significant in the marketing of the level 3 programme as an A level equivalent and therefore an alternative route to Higher Education. Prior to this, the awards were known as level 1, level 2 and level 3. This change raised the profile and perception of the advanced programme. It did not, however, result in an increased esteem for intermediate and foundation programmes. Bathmaker (2002) reported that both students and lecturers recognised that only Advanced GNVQ had any real exchange value outside the college, and Bloomer and Hodkinson (1997) found that students used GNVQ as a gradual progression to get them 'back on track' and eventually to university, inferring that the GNVQ route provided a progression route to Higher Education (after achieving advanced level) rather than entry to the world of work. It seems likely that similar differences in esteem will emerge between specialised Diplomas and GCSEs, particularly where young people achieve a specialised Diploma but not the general (GCSE) diploma which depends on achieving 5 A*-C GCSEs including English and Maths.

There has been a policy assumption that young people can progress through the levels, but this assumes that the ability, willingness and support networks exist for every young person, together with an ultimate aim to progress to Higher Education. Such a perspective also assumes equal potential in all young people in all areas of their life and is dissonant with philosophies of diversity and with the sociological argument that educational achievement is related to social class reproduction (Tomlinson, 2001). In making such an assumption, policy also denies any intrinsic value in education for its own sake at lower levels, or in the value of increased self esteem or self confidence, or other non-pecuniary benefits which might arise from undertaking such a programme (Preston and Hammond, 2003).

Such a policy also renders the needs and aspirations of students at lower levels invisible within the wider policy and education agenda, as they under-take vocational programmes which will not accrue them any esteemed credentials but which Chitty (1991b:104) has suggested may be seen to inculcate the attitudes needed for low skill, low paid work such as punctuality, attendance, time-keeping and discipline. This would enable them, at best, to enter the low skilled, service sector employment regarded by Bathmaker (2001) as the most likely occupational destination for Foundation GNVQ students. The likelihood of vocational students on lower level programmes entering this type of employment was first raised before the introduction of GNVQ when Ainley (1991:103) argued that vocational education is used as a cover for creating a mass of low-paid and semi-skilled casual workers to be used as demand dictates.

Ecclestone (2002:17-19), whilst writing in a different political context, considered that employers' poor record of investment in education and training may form part of a rational strategy linked to low prices, monopolisation and low wages. Not all employers, she suggests, want or need highly skilled workers so that, far from being the idealised situation portrayed by a post-Fordist, high skills rhetoric, the reality of the jobs market facing many post-16 learners is one of unemployment, or low skilled, temporary work with low status training as an alternative to Further or Higher Education.

Concerns also surround the social consequences of the broader structure of the Post Compulsory Education and Training (PCET) sector, as well as aspects of the post-16 curriculum. Tarrant (2001) raised concerns about the structure of vocational education and training arguing that it produces 'a user socialised to work, rather than a citizen'. Whilst Tarrant's concerns relate to wider society, and the ability of all to participate in a democracy, they have resonance with other concerns about the use of vocationalism as a form of social control, and ways in which the structure of vocational programmes generally, and their forms of assessment, may contribute to this. Hargreaves (1989:137) considers that assessment and monitoring procedures have the potential for extreme forms of social surveillance, in which reviews form an 'almost unending process of repeated and regulated assessment' and suppress ''deviant' conduct even before it arises' and Ecclestone (2002) has argued that differentiation may act as a form of social control as it means that the teacher places a lower expectation on some students than on others.

Ambivalent definitions and negative discourse

McCulloch (1998:4), whilst writing more generally about education considered fit for 'the mass of the population' highlights the negative descriptors used to define 'the mass' of young people, from the 'working class' used in Victorian debates to terminology such as 'average and less than average' or 'less able' used in contemporary writing and government documents. Similar types of discourse (low attainers, lacking the minimum basic and employability skills) may be found in current government education policy documents (DfES, 2003a:9, 2003b:24) and are subsequently reflected in the implementation of those policies. Corbett (1999) has discussed the consequences of labelling young people in this way and has argued that:

> What is significant for the [young people] concerned is that, unless they are highly resilient, they are likely to absorb these negative images of themselves and take on the roles of passive victim or social outsider. (Corbett, 1999:181)

Therefore, it may be argued that the discourse relating to these students influences perceptions of them both as individuals and as a cohort, and that this influence is strongly negative.

Despite the range of descriptors outlined above, vocational students form a group which is difficult to define clearly. Level 1 (16-19) is defined as mainstream in some colleges, but placed within Learning Difficulties and Disabilities (LDD) provision in others. In other colleges, level 1 holds a more ambivalent position where it is technically mainstream, but where the stu-

31

dents enrolled on the programme are identified as having additional learning needs, facilitating the funding to provide smaller groups and a higher staff-student ratio, broadly comparable to those found in LDD provision. Bath-maker also highlighted the 'ambivalent positioning of GNVQ Foundation' ; at Midlands College, where she undertook her case study, it was part of the special needs stream but had moved backwards and forwards from mainstream a number of times. Wolf (2002:220), in a study of level 2 students, refers to the *intermediate* qualification as being taken by 'the weakest post GCSE candidates', implying that anything below intermediate would be special needs provision. In 14-16 provision, whilst level 2 forms part of the mainstream provision, many level 1 courses fall within 'alternative curriculum' provision, a term which is often simply a euphemism encompassing those who are deemed to be disaffected or challenging in some way.

The definition of Special Needs or Learning Difficulties and Disabilities provision is much clearer, being based on a formal statement of Special Educational Need which is attached to young people who have received their statutory education within special needs provision. Likewise, those students enrolled on level 2 programmes are more clearly defined, having status both within national government education targets outlined in the Opportunity and Excellence White Paper (DfES, 2003a) and the Skills Agenda (DfES, 2003b). Level 1 provision is more ambivalent, although there is a clear, if unspoken, hierarchy of programmes at this level. At GCSE, a D grade might almost have been a C, and gives a little credibility, particularly in maths and English. A grade G is almost unclassified, and therefore many young people are unwilling to own such a grade. NVQ provision at level 1 provides an opportunity to gain the basic skills needed for a particular type of employment – hairdressing for example – and therefore constitutes a basic training from which the young person can progress to a level 2 qualification and fulfil the requirements of the Governments skills agenda. E2E provision, at the other end of the level 1 spectrum, provides for socially and educationally excluded young people with a wide range of learning and other special needs, such as Emotional and Behavioural Difficulty (EBD), medical problems, history of school exclusion or criminal activity or other social need or difficulty. Those students undertaking broad vocational qualifications at level 1 fall between these groups, in the middle of this spectrum though including elements of each and are, therefore, more difficult to define as a group.

The characteristics that these students do have in common include the fact that, by virtue of being on a low level programme, they have low levels of acdemic credentials in terms of GCSE results, and that most report a poor educational experience pre-16 and significant personal and social difficulties (Ainley and Bailey, 1997:79-80). Ball *et al* (2000) suggest that these young people are constrained in their options by a broad range of factors including social, economic and educational exclusion as well as by the limited educational opportunities available at level 1 post-16 (14-19 Reform Group, 2004a; Bathmaker, 2002). This positioning means that many young people on low level vocational courses are, to draw on Macrae *et al*'s 1997 typology, 'hanging in' to education in the face of significant barriers which are not experienced by their more affluent, middle class peers.

Summary

This chapter has reviewed the positioning of Level 1 and 2 students in the post-16 market place. The existing literature suggests that they are low status students undertaking low status programmes which have ambivalent positioning in the post-16 sector and offer little prospect of achieving more than low pay, low skill employment. Thus, the positioning of these students may be identified as being at the bottom end of an already divisive educational system, in which young people's choices are largely determined by social class and where those undertaking vocational programmes are socialised into particular types of employment.

3

Social justice

Introduction

The theoretical framework which underpinned the research on which this book is based is reflected in one of the original aims of the study: to undertake an inclusive research process informed by a social justice perspective. This chapter explores the concept of social justice in the context of the research project. It is informed by contemporary academic literature as well as by philosophic and religious texts, and by my personal values and beliefs. The concept of justice is an ancient value from which that of social justice is derived. Consequently, it is not a fixed entity nor something which lends itself readily to definition. The chapter begins by considering broader and historical meanings and understandings before moving on to discuss the interpretation of the concept used in the research project and the writing of this book. Alternative interpretations of the term social justice are explored, with particular reference to inequalities in the 14-19 education system in the UK and in the context of a belief in the equal value of each individual.

Social justice: some meanings and interpretations

The notion of social justice, despite existing for thousands of years, remains fragmented and open to debate amongst many 'different voices' (Griffiths, 2003:45). It has been variously described as 'a family of ideas' and an 'abstract universal' (Minogue, 1998:253) and as an 'older moral tradition' by MacIntyre (1981:234) who has also discussed 'rival traditions' (p235) to illustrate the conflicting perceptions of the nature of social justice. These multiple, sometimes conflicting and confused interpretations, meanings and definitions are discussed and then considered in the context of equality and inequality in education.

A 'traditional' view of justice (MacIntyre, 1981:234) is derived from the morality of the early Greek philosophers and ancient Judeo-Christian texts. The Greek philosophers, notably Plato and Aristotle, were amongst the first to debate the notion of justice which is equated with 'human excellence' in Plato's *Republic* (Lee, 1955:15) and defined as 'a moral state' in Aristotle's epic work *The Nicomachean Ethics* (1911/1998:76). Earlier, Biblical writings also make reference to the notion of justice (eg Amos, 5:24) which are initially related to morality and, similarly to the philosophic writings, to the concept of righteousness.

An early concept of social justice is also evident in Aristotle's writings. He discusses the notion of reciprocity, arguing that 'by proportionate reciprocity of action the social community is held together' (1911/1998:84) and continues to debate social relations in the context of justice and injustice (*ibid*: 87). The concept of reciprocity may also be found in the New Testament, which introduces an interpretation of the notion of reciprocity and desert: 'If any would not work, neither should he eat' (2 Thessalonians 3:10). It is perceived as a form of morality in some early philosophic writings: Cephalus, in Plato's *Republic* (1955:3) offers an interpretation in terms of his understanding of justice as 'telling the truth and paying one's debts' whilst Socrates successfully demonstrates that the just man is happier than the unjust, and also argues for a dialogic approach to the concept of justice.

A dialogic, or debated approach or interpretation, has also been advocated by contemporary writers. Griffiths (2003) advocates a dialogic approach to the development of social justice, whilst MacIntyre (1981:236) argues that dialogue and negotiation were fundamental to justice in the absence of a shared set of moral first principles in society. Whilst there may be an absence of shared moral principles, a moral concept of justice is a widely held tradition which is largely shared between Aristotelian philosophers and Christianity (MacIntyre, *ibid*: 235/236). Despite this general agreement that justice has a moral basis, different definitions and interpretations of the term have been evident from the earliest times. This diversity of understanding is eloquently described by MacIntyre (1981:235) in his statement 'Rival conceptions of justice [which are] formed by and informing the life of rival groups'. Thus, history offers insights into the origins of the contemporary lack of clarity in terms of defining the term 'social justice' and illustrates that this concept is highly complex, meaning many different things to many different people.

One aspect of social justice is the concept of the 'common good' which is found in both Aristotelian philosophy and Christian teaching though, yet again, there are differing interpretations. Aristotle argues that 'the greatest good ... is justice, in other words, the common interest' (Aristotle, 1988, *The Politics* III, II. 1282b 15). Hume (1740:318) argued that '[I]t'was therefore a concern for our own, and the public interest, which made us establish the laws of justice' and MacIntyre has discussed the relationship of this philosophic morality to that of Christianity at some length (1981:154-168).

The notion is given prominence in John Paul II's Catechism of the Catholic Church (undated: 421) which argues that 'the conditions that allow associations or individuals to obtain what is their due, according to their nature and their vocation' are essential to achieving social justice, and places a responsibility on the part of society to ensure that the conditions exist to enable individuals to achieve their potential. This belief recognises and values diversity, but is opposed to inequalities associated with the exclusion of people, or a lower value being placed upon them, based on difference. If one group, such as particular types of students, are oppressed or denied opportunity in any way, then this becomes a 'sinful inequality' (John Paul II, undated: 424).

MacIntyre (1981:227-232) discusses the concepts of reciprocity and desert in terms of the distribution of material wealth, the extent to which it can be earned or deserved and the extent to which that material wealth could or should be re-distributed amongst the 'needy'. He also rehearses a number of arguments about why people are affluent or needy, relative to the rest of society. The arguments around reciprocity have been considered by many writers across millennia (for example see St. Paul's letter to the Thessalonians; Hume, 1740: III ii 2:318; Minogue, 1998:258); Rawls (1999:301/308), whilst not addressing reciprocity directly, debates the concept of 'fairness', with which some parallels may be drawn, and Griffiths (in Wallace, 2008:278) argues that social justice 'depends both on respect and also on a right distribution of benefits and responsibilities' .

Social justice has been part of New Labour's mantra since they were first elected in 1997 (Tomlinson, 2005:91) and their commitment to this concept also encompasses a notion of reciprocity. This is apparent in current government education policy (eg DfES, 2003b), where educational opportunities, such as skill-based level 2 programmes, are made available to people in return for the increased economic contribution they will make as a result of having particular skills or credentials. It is most apparent in the rights and responsibilities agenda of New Labour's 'Third Way'.

In the education arena this has resulted in a perception that some individuals require motivating to return to, or to stay in, education, and that this motivation is positive in that it enables individuals to participate, a policy approach which may be seen as coercive. This policy approach also means that young people are participating in a system which, based on perceived economic need, is preparing them for an economic role (eg see DfES, 2006). Accordingly, education has been provided in return for economic contribution, rather than providing opportunities for individuals to undertake learning for less instrumental reasons such as a democratic right or for a common good (Tomlinson, 2005:216).

Debates about the rights or wrongs of reciprocity and the function of education will persist. However, in terms of government policy such a philosophy appears to be fundamentally flawed in that not only is it based on elements of coercion but it also assumes a similar starting point, range and level of opportunity, potential and motivation for each individual to undertake lifelong learning and make the required economic contribution.

Human value and lower level students

Consideration of the human value of each individual, and of notions of equality and inequality, are fundamental to perspectives on social justice. In the context of vocational education courses, particularly those at a lower level which are marketed as offering 'opportunities', it may be argued that the students' learning identities and aspirations are inextricably linked with the (unequal) opportunities that are available to them.

Currently, society places a different value on different individuals according to the characteristics which make them individual. These characteristics reflect the societal and embodied structures which serve to constrain young people's agency. In this way, structures such as class, race, gender, disability as well as perceptions such as potential economic value all become criteria used to judge a person's worth. This notion of value or worth may be extended to the educational programmes undertaken by young people.

Vocational programmes are often held in lower esteem by the educational establishment (Wallace, 2001), are of low value in themselves and largely offered by low status institutions (Colley, 2006:25). The low esteem in which these qualifications are held reflects both the social value that society ascribes to the related occupation and also education and economic policy which places differing values on different types of education and occupation. This view is supported by Robinson's study (1997:35), which found that 'there is no parity of esteem in the labour market'. He bases his arguments on findings from his research which suggest that an individual with an academic qualification (eg A Level) commands an income equivalent to that of another individual with a vocational qualification which is notionally one level higher (eg NVQ level 4).

The notion of individual value being dependent on individual wealth or achievement is not new. Hume, writing in the first half of the 18th Century argued that 'nothing has a greater tendency to give us an esteem for any person than his power and riches; or a contempt, than his poverty and meanness:' (Hume, 1740/2000:231 2.2.5). Others felt that society would be improved if it was based on moral principles associated with respect and equality. Hume's contemporary, the German philosopher Immanuel Kant, who lived from 1724-1804, was deeply concerned with the notion of showing respect for individuals and valuing 'personhood' and discussed morality, immorality and individuals' responsibility for their actions in the context of 'the absolute worth of the human being' (Kant, 2002:57). This respect for humanity is fundamental to Kant's thinking: he believes that it is one of four feelings produced by reason which motivate people to behave in a moral way. He argues that 'both philanthropy and the respect for the rights of humankind are duties. The former is however, only a *conditional* duty, whereas the latter is *unconditional* and absolutely obligatory' (1795/2006:108, original emphasis) and it forms the basis of his categorical imperative: 'act so that you treat humanity, whether in your own person or in that of another, always as an end and never as a means only' (2002:xviii).

In more contemporary society, this argument is ongoing and unchanged. In 1966 Abbot and Gallagher argued that '...the basic equality of all must receive increasingly greater recognition' and in 1981 MacIntyre was arguing for the treatment of others based on uniform, impersonal standards (1981:179). Later, Griffiths, in the second of her three principles for social justice argued that 'each individual is valuable and [should be] acknowledged as such by wider society' (1998:12/13) and more recently (in Wallace, 2008:277-279) she discusses the concept of respect for others in the context of social justice. However, despite these longstanding arguments, both wider society and the education system remain divided and inequitable with very different opportunities – or lack of them – available to young people based largely on social status, highlighting Bourdieu's (2000:214/215) argument that 'Those who talk of equality of opportunity forget that social games ... are not 'fair games".

Bourdieu's theories on structure and agency, habitus and field and capital, all of which relate to his primary concern of inequality within society, provide a useful framework for understanding the injustices imposed by social, educational and political structures on students taking vocational courses. They also provide the opportunity to develop an understanding which avoids 'a polarised explanation focused either on social structures or individual free choice' (Hodkinson, 1998:100). This understanding provides a basis from which to consider ways of challenging and addressing those inequities.

Bourdieu and Wacquant define the field as 'a configuration of relations between positions objectively defined, in their existence and in the determinations they impose upon the occupants, agents or institutions' (1992a:72-73) and use the analogy of sport to explain the meaning of the concept, describing the 'feel for the game' that enables a footballer to anticipate what might happen next, and the different ways in which the game is controlled and structured. Likewise, they argue that individuals are 'born into' social fields and learn the 'symbolic capital' of that field – unwritten rules, cultural beliefs and practices, language – necessary to survive and succeed in that field. Grenfell and James (1998:20) identify education as a field consisting of interconnecting, identifiable relations. Within this field, vocational and academic education may be regarded as sub-fields.

It has been argued that vocational education is class specific (Colley *et al*, 2003) and the debate around parity of esteem for vocational education illustrates the low status of vocational programmes in comparison to academic programmes (eg McCulloch, 1998; Wallace, 2001). Therefore there are clear power differentials between the subfields of vocational and academic education where vocational education is regarded as inferior, and even within that field clear hierarchies exist between different academic levels. Within these hierarchies, in terms of both level and type of qualification, level 1 vocational programmes have no academic or vocational credibility and form the bottom rung of the mainstream 14-19 educational hierarchy, particularly in the post-16 phase. The position for level 2 students is little better as programmes at this level simply provide a progression route to level 3. Level 3 students have, perhaps, most credibility in this field, but they are less likely to access Higher Education successfully and more likely to attend less selective Higher Education Institutions (Hoelscher and Hayward, 2008:20).

As the young people on these low level programmes make the transition to a higher level of further education or into the world of work, each new setting or organisation to which they progress will have its own unwritten code of behaviour, manners and linguistics. Success in that field will depend partly on the individual's ability to absorb and unconsciously comply with those codes.

Bourdieu uses notions of habitus and field to explain those of structure and agency. Structure relates to social structures, ie any external environment that is seen to be set apart from, or controlling and influencing, the actions of agents or individuals. Examples of such structures would be social class, the family, education and the state; however, the concept may also be used to consider embodied structures engendered by characteristics such as race, disability and gender which can determine and reproduce how people think and behave, characteristics which are 'constitutive of, rather than determined by, social structures' (Reay, 1998:61).

Ways in which individuals think and behave may also be explained by the concept of habitus, which relates to their primary knowledge of their life and situation and to their 'inheritance of the accumulated experiences of their antecedents' (Robbins, 1998:35) and crucially, is embodied rather than consisting of attitudes and perceptions (Reay, 1995:117). Habitus is durable (Bourdieu and Passeron, 1977;1990:33) but also subject to change over time, a process which Bourdieu describes as 'transform[ing] the habitus' (Bourdieu, 1980c, 1993a:87).

Agency may be defined as the ability that agents (individuals) have to control their own actions or destiny within those structures and, as such, the concept is related to choice and subjective motivation. In this way, the field 'orients choices' (Bourdieu, 1990:66), but individual agency will determine which of those choices are made and this will in turn be influenced by the habitus of the individual, their motivation and values as, particularly in the case of lower level students, they 'struggle to make the world a different place' (Reay, 2004: 437).

For lower level vocational students, individual agency is heavily restricted by the structures of the state, society and the education system which 'serve to reproduce inequality' (Avis, 2007:162-167). In terms of the state, they are constrained by government policy, both economic and educational, which 'orients choice' by determining the vocational nature of the limited curriculum available to them (Working Group on 14-19 Reform, 2003, 2004a). External structures such as the education system and societal attitudes mean that those programmes are held in low esteem and do not provide a clear route or preparation for employment. In terms of society, the young people inhabit a field pre-determined by social class and local culture or habitus, as well as embodied structures such as disability, gender and race which result in less access to cultural capital (Reay, 1998:56).

Therefore, in respect of developing learning identities and negotiating successful transitions to the world of work, these young people are constrained by multiple barriers and, however well motivated or however determined to 'transform the habitus' (Bourdieu, 1980c, 1993a:87), the options available to them are very limited. Their learning programmes will not provide an occupational qualification leading to the argument that low level vocational programmes are preparing students only for low pay, low skill work (Bathmaker, 2001).

Educational progression routes are no less restrictive, as those available lead entirely to vocationalised programmes. Achieving a craft or professional qualification will mean an extended transition period requiring determination, motivation, financial capital and parental interest and support. Predestination to certain types of education and job roles, and the reproduction of class membership in this way is illustrated in Bourdieu and Passeron's model, *The educational career and its system of determinations*. This model suggests that the 'objective probabilities' of particular trajectories are primarily determined by social class, though also influenced by factors such as gender and geography (see Bourdieu and Passeron, 1977, 1990).

The position of lower level vocational students, where they are denied access to resources, treated as inferior and limited in their aspiration and social mobility (Webb *et al*, 2002:25) may be perceived as a form of symbolic violence (Bourdieu and Passeron, 1977/1990:67). Symbolic violence is that which is 'visited on people in a symbolic, rather than a physical way and may take the form of people being denied resources, treated as inferior or being limited in terms of realistic aspirations' (Webb *et al*, 2002:xvi). The victims of symbolic violence such as this do not recognise it for what it is, since these are situations which are socially and culturally embedded. Instead, they regard their situation to be part of 'the natural order of things' and accept it as such.

Deficit models and dependence

In addition to embodied and societal structural forces constraining the agency of many vocational learners, there are other subtle inequalities which impact on their ability to exercise their agency. These include the deficit models which frame our perceptions of many of these young people, as well as the discourse of fragility and the policy context surrounding them and the strategies used in their educational support.

There is rising concern that the uncritical use of therapeutic educational interventions such as circle time or personalised learning in education is leading to a 'diminished self' (Ecclestone, 2004, 2007) – individuals who are disempowered and whose potential for agency is reduced by the well intentioned but uncritical discourse of fragility and the implementation of pseudo-therapeutic interventions in schools and colleges. A broad range of initiatives which might be described as therapeutic in nature are used in further education colleges on a daily basis. These include initiatives such as learning styles questionnaires, personalised learning, and services such as counselling which are routinely available to students in the sector. Other practices such as the focus on improving self-esteem have become embedded throughout the sector, leading Kristjansson, in his critique of such approaches, to observe somewhat wryly that it has been 'touted as the Balm of Gilead ... for quite a while' (2007:247). However, these perspectives have been contested by Hyland (2006:299), who, writing with specific reference to VET policy and practice in the UK, suggests that 'an attention to the important values dimension of learning in the field does involve a therapeutic dimension of some kind'.

The students in this study were all enrolled on 14-19 programmes in colleges of further education and were all undertaking some form of vocational education and training. Those young people entering further education tend to be 14-16 year olds pursuing an alternative (vocational) curriculum, or school leavers with few or no qualifications. Such young people are deemed to be 'at risk' (see Ecclestone and Hayes, 2008, for an extended discussion) and, as such, fit within the deficit models described by Major (1990:23), Colley (2003:4) and Ecclestone (2004, 2007) in the context of policy and provision for socially excluded young people. A discourse of fragility, using terms such as 'disadvantaged', 'disaffected' and 'low achieving' is used to describe this group of learners who are then perceived to need support to overcome these difficulties. As a consequence of this colleges of further education provide a whole raft of support services to address students' perceived needs, whether these are educational, behavioural, social or emotional, and concepts such as personalised learning have entered Government policy as part of central initiatives to address perceived problems of disengagement and disaffection across the 14-19 phase.

These perceptions and initiatives reflect the way many 14-19 vocational learners are othered by Government, academics and society at large. Where groups are othered this means that they are treated as being different in nature or kind from other groups of people, usually because they are excluded or disadvantaged in some way. Fine *et al* (2000:117) argue that our constructions of the other 'however seemingly benevolent and benign' must inevitably influence our perceptions and interpretations. In the case of lower level 14-19 vocational students, the representations of them tend to form two personas. The first of these is the disaffected, disruptive, ineducable youth, reflected in the type of discourse argued by Colley (2003:28) to pathologise those at risk of social exclusion; the second is the representation of these young people as passive, needy victims of circumstance, a therapeutic perception argued by Ecclestone (2004) to diminish the self and erode individual autonomy.

Ecclestone's argument is supported by earlier work. Kant, writing in 1785, argued that 'autonomy is thus the ground of the dignity of the human and of every rational nature' (1785, 1999:54) and more recently Minogue (1998:258) has suggested that a person defined in terms of need must necessarily be construed within a deficit model and so be unable to participate in 'reciprocal human transactions'. He goes on to argue that this is recognised by social justice theorists and obscured by the use of the concept of right which is then extended to universal right. He suggests that this reduces the whole population to a form of dependence on the state and concludes that 'rights are a Greek gift' because they are, in fact, 'an instrument of subjection'.

These are important arguments within a broader social justice context. Specifically in terms of education, however, there are correlations between Minogue's concept of dependence on the state, and Ecclestone and Hayes's (2008:viii/ix) notion of a rising therapeutic culture in education. The book develops Ecclestone's earlier (2004:133) notion of the 'diminished self' in which educational 'failure' is perceived to endow a form of emotional trauma or need, rather than being regarded socially and politically as 'outcomes of an education system that uses assessment to rank and segregate people for unequal opportunities'. Such a state of diminished self may be reflective of a wider social move towards a therapeutic culture which seeks to exercise social control by 'cultivating a sense of vulnerability, powerlessness and dependence' (Furedi, 2004:203).

Furedi goes on to suggest that the 'diminished self' would be less able to exercise the 'citizens' powers of practical reason and thought in forming, revising and rationally pursuing their conception of the good' and hence would be less likely to achieve a more just society (*Ibid*: 203/4). Such citizens would also be less able to engage in the dialogical process which Griffiths (2003) argues is essential within a society which claims to be working towards a state of social justice and which Rawls (1999) assumes all have the capacity to engage in, ultimately leading to an even more inequitable state of society. Minogue

(1998:265) has argued that only a 'completely de-moralised and therapeutic conception of human life' can arise from treating people as creatures with needs to be managed, and foresees a perception that life should be nothing more than a series of pleasant experiences. He uses this to argue against the concept of social justice which he regards as 'a reactionary project for a managed society'. However, Ecclestone perceives arguments for social justice to be a constructive response to the effects of this therapeutic ethos, arguing that 'Demoralised humanism is therefore one of the most pressing problems facing educators and policy makers committed to social justice and the transforming potential of education' (2004:133). In Ecclestone's argument, 'demoralisation' is an 'ethical, philosophical and political' concept which alludes both to a general loss of morale and to a societal loss of confidence and inability to deal with deeper moral dilemmas, leading to diminished human beings (Ecclestone and Hayes, 2008:137; these concerns are developed further in Part 3 of this book).

A vision of social justice

A societal structure which facilitates each individual to achieve their potential in each area of their life may be regarded as an unattainable utopian vision. However, Griffiths (in Wallace, 2008:278) has argued that it is because social justice is unattainable that it should be regarded as a 'process' that we are working towards, and Avis (1996:82) believes that the 'struggle for a more humane society is ... unending'. Any argument for equity in education must accept this as the ultimate aim of a just society, no matter how romantic or unattainable that may appear. In the context of work and education, all young people would be able to access a critical and democratic curriculum which prepared them for lives as active citizens, able to make critical contributions in the workplace, rather than being socialised into particular types of work within a highly stratified society. Such a position would necessarily be underpinned by an equal respect for each individual arising from their status as a person, which recognises and values fundamental differences in terms of interest, aptitude and ambition but which is not associated with any material, intellectual or other perceived benefits and advantages.

The dilemma arising from the vision of an equitable society is that, because of the current nature of society and its structures, and the flaws inherent within the human race, it is never likely to be realised. Like the notion of radical democracy (Zournazi, 2002), a form of politics that recognises diversity, and invites participation from a variety of social spaces in an ongoing process of democratisation, it is something to be struggled towards, rather than something which is attainable. However, this does not make that vision any less valid, since it provides a moral philosophy emphasising the value of and respect for others which forms a basis for dialogue around injustice, and a framework from which it is possible to challenge inequality and debate and 'continually struggle over' (Avis, 1996:82) the best means for addressing it. It may be argued that inherent in subscription to any philosophy, moral or otherwise, is the implication and requirement that any personal actions should reflect these values and beliefs.

A social justice philosophy therefore imposes a moral imperative to act in accordance with the expressed values of that philosophy. This imperative to respond is emphasised by Griffiths (2003:55) when she says: 'Social Justice is a **verb**' (original emphasis) and by Walker (see Griffiths, 2003:125) who argues that 'only through doing justice can we make justice'.

In terms of the issues raised in this book, the way of 'doing justice' is twofold: firstly, a particular stance is taken in the writing, as a response to the impera- tive to acknowledge and explore inequality, and to challenge situations, sys- tems and structures which promote inequality and conflict with the values of social justice. Secondly, in translating this philosophy into practical terms, the methodology for the study used a range of strategies designed to demonstrate value and respect for the young people who participated. This involved trying to use a collaborative approach which facilitated the young people's involve- ment in all aspects of the study from planning to data interpretation. Also fundamental to this was to attempt to represent their 'little stories' (Griffiths, 2003:81) with integrity. I termed this approach 'researching with, not on'.

Researching *with*, not *on*
The wish to research with and not on arose from moral and ethical concerns about social justice, and more technical concerns about the validity of em- pirical research in which the interpretation of data is exclusively that of the re- searcher but is represented as the truth about a particular group. The power in the researcher/participant relationship is inevitably with the researcher, who often inhabits a very different social and political context to that of the participants and, in turn, this can increase the oppression of the participants through specific gendered or class based interpretations of the research pro- cess and data. This is particularly the case where other participants in the research are from traditionally oppressed groups, such as women, those with disabilities or people from specific ethnic groups with a history of oppression. It may be argued that those students pursuing low level vocational pro- grammes form a group which experiences oppression at many levels.

Despite living within a so-called democracy, these young people are stigmatised, and structurally and institutionally oppressed in terms of their social class, gender, racial group, perceived academic ability determined by level of credential, by caring responsibilities, by social perception and in some cases by disability. Each young person who agreed to participate in this research reflected an individual but multi-faceted case of multiple oppressions which in many cases resulted in exclusion from mainstream society. This exclusion is reinforced by a government which pursues what Tomlinson (2005:216) has described as 'special policies' for those 'unlikely or unable to join the economy at any but the very lowest levels'. In this context, where social justice is redefined as forms of policy which promote credentialism whilst failing to recognise any value in low level credentials, and which also utilise a deficit model of social exclusion described by Colley (2003:169) as attributing only perceived negative qualities to people who are categorised in this way, the holder of such low level credentials becomes increasingly devalued as a member of society.

To research with, and not on, formed part of a response to this problem of the politics of power and the degree of exclusion and discrimination experienced by lower level vocational students. Fine (1994) has argued that intellectuals carry a responsibility to engage with struggles for democracy and justice whilst Griffiths (1998:114/115) outlines different forms of collaborative relationship (ie researching with, not on), of 'joint theorising and action' within the context of the power of agency. She argues that such relationships are a means for developing empowerment, voice and ultimately social justice. The participatory approach developed in this research has been, in part, an attempt to respond to these arguments. This involved a re-thinking of the relationship with the young people who participated in the research, and consideration of ways in which a more collaborative and empowering relationship could be engendered, such as developing the more dialogical process advocated by Gitlin and Russell (1994:184).

Summary
This chapter has attempted to unpick the often conflicting and confused notions of social justice and offer an interpretation of the meaning of the term. In doing this it has illustrated the frameworks – theoretical, practical, moral and philosophical – which inform contemporary debates and understandings of social justice and associated concepts and has explored contemporary concerns around the diminished self and therapeutic education which may be regarded as contrary to social justice.

Part 2
Narratives of a difficult present, hopes for a different future

I was told that the Privileged and the People formed Two Nations (Disraeli,1845)

Part two of this book is presented as four chapters. The first is a brief discussion of the social and institutional contexts of the two institutions which participated in the study, and provides an outline of the type of curriculum followed by the students at the time the fieldwork was undertaken. The following three chapters are individual narratives of each of the student groups who participated in the study.

4

The social and institutional contexts of the colleges

Introduction

Students and staff from two geographically distant colleges participated in this study. These were Woodlands College in Midport in the
Midlands and St. Dunstan's College in Townsville in the North of
England. This chapter provides an outline of the similarities between them in
terms of their social and economic context and the student population they
serve and describes their different approaches to level one provision, also
highlighting the limitations of the curriculum on offer to young people at this
level.

The following three chapters present the data from this study as individual
narratives of each of the three groups who participated. *Visions of a Digital
Future* relates to the young people undertaking a GNVQ foundation IT course
at St. Dunstan's College. *Rehearsing Domesticity* describes the lives of the
young women undertaking GNVQ foundation Health and Social Care at the
same college, and *Serving Time* narrates the stories of the young people
undertaking a locally designed level 1/2 course at Woodlands College.

Although each group is considered separately, data analysis found broad
similarities across the three groups relating primarily to social class, gender
and leisure, and these themes are reflected in the sub-headings used for each
chapter. They reflect the difficulties experienced by these young people in
many areas of their lives, and the hopes that they have for a different kind of
future. In order to give a clear context to each narrative, each chapter begins
with a brief profile of the student group concerned and all conclude with a
brief summary of the key themes arising from the data.

St. Dunstan's College

St. Dunstan's College is a large General Further Education College. It has two campuses which are several miles apart. This study took place at the main site, which is located in the centre of Townsville, an industrial town in northern England. Educational achievement and raising aspiration in young people are major concerns in Townsville and the surrounding areas. The borough experiences significant social disadvantage across all areas of measurement according to the government's Indices of Multiple Deprivation (Department of Communities and Local Government, Indices of Deprivation 2007 available at: http://www.communities.gov.uk/communities/neigh-bourhoodrenewal/deprivation/deprivation07/). Achievement rates at GCSE are below the national average, although these have improved in recent years as a result of major investment in the 14-19 agenda by the LEA. In 2007 39 per cent of young people in the Local Authority gained 5 or more A*-C GCSEs including English and Maths, compared with a national average of 46.8 per cent . Attainment at key stage 3 as well as key stage 4 in 2007 was well below the national average, despite being the highest in the sub-region and improving. Aspiration amongst young people in Townsville has also been identified as a cause for concern and progression to Higher Education is poor despite considerable investment in increasing and widening participation by the College and the LEA. Sub-regional data for 2006 indicated that nearly 11 per cent of young people were disengaged and not in education, employment or training.

These issues have their roots in the sudden and massive industrial decline which hit the town during the 1980s, and in the work and cultural practices which preceded it. Until then most young men entered employment in the mines, steelworks or their servicing industries. There was also full employment for young women, although job roles were split on strictly gender lines, a situation which is still evident in labour market participation analyses (Objective One, undated:133). Between 1981 and 1995 this security vanished, as employment fell by 90 per cent in the mining industry and by 24 per cent in the manufacturing industries, coinciding with a sub-regional fall of 20 per cent in all jobs (Objective One undated:16). There was little tradition of higher education in the town, although historically it had some well respected grammar schools and, unusually for a town of some 250,000 people, three Further Education Colleges and one Sixth Form College. The Further Education Colleges, two of which have since merged, were originally founded to support the mining industry whilst the Sixth Form College derives from a medieval Grammar School Foundation.

Education partnership work within the borough has involved the learning partnership, education and training providers, the LEA and local universities, focusing on the development of alternative, mainly vocational post-14 routes which are related to local economic needs and are perceived to be more likely to engage young people. The College is central to these partnerships, offering lower level vocational programmes for 14-19 students in partnership with schools, and widening participation Higher Education programmes in partnership with local universities. These initiatives were originally a response to the local Area Wide Inspection Action Plan, and government policy as expressed in the Green Paper (DfES, 2002) and are ongoing in response to the Government's 14-19 Agenda. Simultaneously, European money has supported regeneration in the town and industries based on new technologies are now developing.

St. Dunstan's College has worked closely with schools, other providers and local employers to provide relevant training for young people wishing to enter these occupational areas and in some areas is able to provide pathways from level 1 to HND. The GNVQ Foundation was, until its withdrawal, a cornerstone of level 1 provision in the college. It has now been replaced with the BTEC Introductory Diploma. Two GNVQ foundation groups participated in the study, one in IT and one in Health and Social Care.

Woodlands College

Woodlands College is a large General Further Education College located on multiple campuses across Midport, a city in the English Midlands. According to government indices of multiple deprivation (Department of Communities and Local Government, Indices of Deprivation 2007 available at: http://www.communities.gov.uk/communities/neighbourhoodrenewal/deprivation/deprivation07/) the city has amongst the highest levels of social deprivation in England, much of which is a consequence of the decline of the city's industrial base during the late 20th Century. Consequently, the levels and extent of disadvantage amongst the Woodlands student population are higher than those in Townsville.

Although increasing regeneration is now evident, this is less advanced than that in Townsville. GCSE League tables suggest that, in terms of the educational achievement of school leavers the city is one of the lowest achieving in England. In 2007, only 33 per cent of year 11 students gained five or more GCSE grades at A* – C including English and Maths, compared with 46.8 per cent nationally, although this figure masks wide variations between different institutions. Similarly, KS3 Attainment is well below national averages, despite significant improvements over the past three years. Participation in post-16 education is well below the national average and a large proportion of young people enter employment without training.

As a result of this situation, at the time the fieldwork for this study was undertaken, approximately 45 per cent of enrolments at Woodlands College were to level 1 programmes, and concerns about the value of the curriculum offer at this level had led the college to develop its own level 1 provision. This was based on some vocational education supported by basic skills and short courses, each of which was individually accredited. A phased implementation of this provision began in 2005.

As well as the development of a broader offer at level 1, the college has established a wide range of partnerships with organisations such as community learning providers, charities, social services and the probation service to try to address issues of low achievement and extend opportunities for learning. Similarly to St. Dunstan's College, it has also established a broad range of partnerships with schools to provide Increasing Flexibility (IFP) and related vocational programmes for 14-19 students. This, and the developing level 1 provision, forms part of the College response to educational and social inclusion in the significantly disadvantaged areas that it serves.

Differences and similarities – the problematisation of level 1 students

Whilst there are significant differences between the two organisations, there are also marked similarities. Both Colleges, though geographically distant from one another, are in areas which suffered significantly from the industrial decline of the late 20th Century. Both serve broadly similar student groups and both are actively developing their 14-19 provision. However, each organisation has made a different response to the perceived problems of lower level students.

St. Dunstan's College has concentrated on offering a generic Entry or foundation level programme from which students may progress to a broad range of level 1 BTEC qualifications (Foundation GNVQ at the time of this study) and subsequently to higher levels in each vocational area. Woodlands College, however, has developed a generic level 1 programme, located within a separate department, from which students may progress to mainstream level 2 courses across the college. Both approaches have disadvantages: the range of nationally accredited level 1 awards is limited, and whilst there were plans to extend it, the level 1 provision at Woodlands College offered just four vocational options in the year this study took place.

A further similarity between the two colleges is that Level 1 students are problematised within both organisations, in the sense that they represent, collectively or individually, problems to be solved. This problematising is evident institutionally and at departmental and individual lecturer level, sometimes overt, but more often covert in terms of the discourse used and the expectations of the young people, and can be seen to reflect policy approaches and public and media perceptions. For example, staff overtly discuss 'progression'. In doing this they reinforce government assumptions about straightforward transitions and lifelong learning, whilst covertly acknowledging that for many of their students this is an unlikely option.

The problematisation of the students did not appear to be recognised by the tutors who participated in the study, all of whom were enthusiastic and expressed deep commitment to a student group whom they perceived to be significantly disadvantaged. It was apparent that the problematisation of the young people co-existed within a strong nurturing ethos, and that the nurturing approach was perceived by the tutors to be the best approach to resolving the students' perceived difficulties. The nurturing approach reflected some gender differences (it was more evident in two groups with a predominantly female staff group), but was most apparent in the Health and Social Care group, perhaps also influenced by the professional backgrounds of the lecturers on the programme.

GNVQ Foundation and the Level 1 programme: structure and content

Two groups of learners were following GNVQ foundation programmes. Now replaced by the BTEC Introductory Diploma, the foundation included six very broad units of study which covered generalised topics such as employment in the sector. In Health and Social Care at level 1 the unit covering employment was called 'Investigating Health and Social Care' and involved exploring the job roles found in the Health, Care and Childcare sectors. A typical assessment would be to research the responsibilities and qualifications associated with a range of job roles across these sectors, and present them as a portfolio. This might involve brief (one paragraph) information about three or four job roles in each sector. The Introductory Diploma has a similar unit which, in addition to the sectors covered in the GNVQ, requires coverage of the Youth Service sector and looks at job roles across the EU as well as in the UK. The very broad requirements of units of study at this level indicate that any knowledge gained can only be at the most superficial level.

The GNVQ had a requirement that Key Skills, including the wider Key Skills such as 'working as a member of a team', were embedded in the programme. The Key Skills were mapped into students' assessed work by tutors to show coverage and achievement. GNVQ assessment was more formal. Two units were assessed by external examination in the form of short answer papers, and four by written assignment such as that described above. The introduction of externally assessed exams as a result of the Curriculum 2000 reforms was significant as the high pass mark made it difficult for students to achieve Merit or Distinction in the exams, and the final, overall grade was based on an average of the marks awarded for each unit. Therefore, of those students who passed the award, a majority did so with a Pass rather than a higher grade.

The IT GNVQ incorporated assessments which reflected the technological content of the course. Consequently, one assessment for the IT group in this study was to produce a PowerPoint presentation about their GNVQ course: examples of slides of one of these PowerPoints are included in this book and may be found on pages 83/84.

The course involved sixteen hours per week attendance at college for one academic year, which currently equates to full time education post-16. Marketing of the programme by colleges emphasised progression and opportunities reflecting Government rhetoric about vocational education, even where those opportunities were, to say the least, illusory. One advert by a college unrelated to those in the study included the following:

Future Opportunities

This qualification helps you to go to higher level qualifications, such as AVCEs or A levels or a (sic) Intermediate GNVQ in Health and Social care. Alternatively you can go straight into work. This GNVQ Foundation course prepares you for a wide range of career opportunities in the field of Health and Social Care.

Figure 1: College on-line marketing 2005

The level 1 course at Woodlands covered a similar, prescriptive curriculum, albeit in smaller chunks which offered individual accreditation and a choice of vocational option. The vocational option involved working towards NVQ level 1 units on one day per week. At the time the fieldwork for this book was carried out, only four options were available; however, the programme was in its early stages and there were plans to increase this in subsequent years. The young people pursued the vocational option in the department which provided it, and spent the remainder of their time in college in the level 1 centre, where the rest of the provision was located. This time was spent with the level 1 staff team working on basic literacy and numeracy skills and Personal and Social Education (PSE) and accruing a range of small credentials from Entry to Level 2. Like the GNVQ Foundation, the Level 1 was a full time programme requiring attendance of sixteen hours a week. However, it was not timetabled as strictly as the rest of the college. In recognition of the students' perceived needs, staff reported that they could adjust lessons or rooms if necessary, in order to meet those needs more effectively.

Summary

This chapter has provided a brief social and economic context for each of the institutions which participated in the research and has illustrated the levels of educational disadvantage experienced by the populations they serve. It has also considered the ways in which young people on vocational education programmes are problematised, and outlined the structure and content of the programmes followed by the students who participated in the study, in order to provide a context for the narratives which follow. These narratives suggest that, whilst some of the young people might have met the formal outcomes dictated by these programmes, they were also learning other things. Some of these were associated with identity formation, particularly where this related to social and leisure activity, and some were associated with the hidden curriculum which was preparing them for particular roles in life.

5

Visions of a digital future: GNVQ IT group, St. Dunstan's College

Introduction -

This narrative reports on the GNVQ Foundation (Information Technology) group at St. Dunstan's College. These young people, despite undertaking a programme which taught the most basic computer operating skills (eg use of the internet and PowerPoint), anticipated affluent futures where that affluence would be generated by high status employment within the digital economy.

Group profile

The GNVQ Foundation group studying Information Technology at St. Dunstan's College consisted of twelve students, and eight of these participated in the study. The students were aged between 16 and 20 and all came from more disadvantaged areas of Townsville. Seven of the participating students were male, and only one, Emma, was female. Emma withdrew from the programme at the end of term one. Four students, Naz, Amir, Abdul and Samir described their ethnicity as Pakistani or Asian, and four – Al, Wayne, Pete and Emma – described their ethnicity as English or British. This is not reflective of the ethnic mix in the borough where, according to the 2001 census, only 2.2 per cent of the population was Asian (Office for National Statistics, 2006).

Educational achievement in the town in 2004 (the year most of this group took GCSEs) was below the national average, with 46 per cent achieving 5 GCSEs at A*-C grade in comparison with 53.7 per cent nationally (DCSF, 2008). Inevitably, one outcome of below average GCSE outcomes is that larger numbers of young people progress to low level further education programmes, rather than to higher level programmes offering better educational and employment opportunities.

One of the group, Samir, was not enrolled on the GNVQ foundation but was doing part of the programme as infill from the pre-level one provision. He had been educated in special schools, had a physical disability and used a wheelchair. Samir was present for all the data gathering activities and participated in them enthusiastically. The group was taught by three key staff members: Nick, the programme coordinator, and Neil and Sara, who were both lecturers on the programme. All three were interviewed as part of this study.

The students were asked to describe their families' occupational and educational backgrounds, and the results are summarised in figure 2 opposite. Sibling gender is given where this was provided by the student. In other cases, the young people referred to 'brothers and sisters'.

The data in figure 2 is represented in the way it was described by each student. It was apparent that, where occupation was known to the student, all employed parents were in low-paid, working class specific occupations. This was also the case for most siblings, although Naz had two sisters who were both at university, and Abdul reported having 'cousins with degrees'. In addition to the class specificity evident in parental occupations, it was also apparent that where the mothers were engaged in paid employment, their occupations were all also gender typical, as were those of the siblings who were in paid employment. This strongly gendered pattern extended to the programme which the students were undertaking. Only one female student was enrolled during the year in which this study was conducted, reflecting a phenomenon which is also present in technology based occupations where 80 per cent of the employees are male (Office for National Statistics, 2002).

Imagined futures

During their interviews the young people were asked 'what sort of job would you like to do in the future?' and, to establish whether or not they had a role model for this, they were also asked whether they already knew anyone who was doing this job. Their answers showed that they had imagined futures in two related areas – occupational aspirations and lifestyle aspirations. These varied, but all the young people emphasised the importance of getting a 'good' job, and only Abdul was not able to be specific about the type of job role he aspired to (see figure 3). Lifestyle aspirations were less variable but, rather than complementing the occupational plans of the young people, there were significant tensions between the two.

Student	Mother's Occupational Background	Father's Occupational Background	Siblings' Occupational/ Educational Background
Samir	House cleaning	Unemployed	1. 'married off' – Housewife 2. 'at home' (?Unemployed) sister 3. Schoolchild (brother) 4. Schoolchild (brother)
Wayne	Cleaner with local MBC	1st Aid Trainer (step-father; father deceased)	1. Plasterer (brother) 2. Joiner (brother) 3. Mechanic (brother)
Al	Not Known	Not Known	1. Schoolchild (sister)
Pete	Deceased	Not in contact	1. Occupation unknown (brother) 2. Schoolchild, in care 3. Schoolchild, in care 4. Schoolchild, in care 5. Schoolchild, in care 6. Schoolchild, in care
Naz	Phlebotomist	Bricklayer	1. Leeds University – Music (sister) 2. Leeds University – Psychology (sister)
Amir	Housewife	Shop assistant	1. Schoolchild 2. Schoolchild 3. Schoolchild
Abdul	Housewife	Not Known	1. Schoolchild 2. Schoolchild 3. Schoolchild 4. Cousins have degrees
Emma	Cleaner	Not in contact	1. Cleaner (sister) 2. Packer (brother)

Figure 2: Occupational and educational backgrounds of IT students' parents and siblings

Student	Occupational Aspiration	Do you know anyone doing what you aspire to?
Samir	Receptionist	No
Wayne	Salesman	No
Al	IT specialist	No
Pete	RAF Ground Crew	Grandfather ex-RAF
Naz	Computer Programmer	Cousin
Amir	Computer Programmer	No
Abdul	Something with computers	No
Emma	Fitness Instructor	No

Figure 3: IT students' occupational aspirations and potential role models

Of eight students, only two had a relative, friend or acquaintance already employed in a related area and four of the group had occupational plans with, at best, a tenuous link to an IT credential. There was a further conflict between the students' occupational plans and their lifestyle aspirations, and the difference between these was so significant as to be incongruous. The students had lifestyle aspirations which fell in the realms of fantasy – acknowledged by Al who wanted to be 'an IT specialist – in America or Japan'. He hoped that the lifestyle which would accompany this would include 'a big mansion in America, tons of girls' but a brief note of reality crept in when he added 'I don't think it's going to come true – I can dream it'.

The tutors' perceptions of the students' futures were framed exclusively within the context of a pursuit of higher and higher rungs of an IT based educational ladder. Generally, the tutors regarded the course as the beginning of a progression route, and considered that its value was as the 'foundation' of an educational ladder which would provide a wider range of career opportunities although they acknowledged that in excess of 20 per cent of the intake probably would not 'progress' from level 1. Despite this, the tutors were unaware of the destinations of the students although Nick speculated that 'some move onto other areas, try something else, or some maybe do get jobs' and Neil considered that

> ...a natural route for them is to go from the foundation onto the intermediate and then higher really. But I think foundation's ...

> it's not a kindergarten that's the wrong thing but it's like it's preparing them for the next [level].

For the students, the future consisted of lifestyle and occupational ambitions, and an educational route to achieving this seemed to be incidental to most of the group. For some, particularly the four students from the Pakistani community, marriage and a family formed a significant aspect of their (more pragmatic) expectations for the future. The other four students in the group came from white British backgrounds. This group of students had strong roots in the local former steelwork, former mining working class community and included Emma, the only female member of the class. Emma had modest plans compared to the rest of the group in that she hoped to work in a gym and to own her own home and she believed that completing the GNVQ Foundation IT and later a Leisure and Tourism Intermediate GNVQ would enable her to achieve them. Despite these clear long term plans, Emma withdrew at the end of the first term.

Wayne was the only white British student to include a family as part of his imagined future. For Wayne, in contrast to the Asian students, this seemed to be a hope rather than an expectation. 'I'll be living with my girlfriend and probably having a baby and getting married and stuff like that'. He expected to be 'dressed up smartly and walking about't streets hoping that people will buy stuff off you because you're that good a salesman'. His ambition to be a salesman conflicted with his lifestyle ambitions, which in themselves held elements of contradiction. He anticipated '[looking after] the baby and my girlfriend as well ... [living] somewhere where it's hot all the time. Where it's beautiful but not like a foreign place'.

Living abroad was a common theme amongst the wider group and most of those who expressed this ambition hoped to live somewhere exotic, with the exception of Naz who intended to move to Germany. He did not have a clear reason for this, but expected to 'marry a German wife' and thought that once in Germany he would 'be a computer programmer'. He thought that he might have to go to university for two years before he could be a computer programmer but expected that he would find the transition to university and the experience there 'easy'. Only Abdul, who had several cousins with degrees, recognised that it would take 'a very long time' to achieve a university education, given a starting point of GNVQ foundation. Samir also mentioned university, in a rather wistful acknowledgement that this would not be part of his own transition: 'I know I can't go to university [because] they have exams, very long exams. After their exams they can do anything they want to'.

Considered in terms of Ball *et al*'s 'arenas of action, centres of choice' (2000: 148), all these young people expressed a significant investment in their education, though other comments they made contradicted this. They demonstrated a more significant investment in their leisure and social life and those students from Asian backgrounds also showed a heavy investment in their cultural and family life. Each of the male Asian students negotiated effectively between these arenas, with little evidence of the dissonance experienced between social and cultural/domestic identities by one young female 'Britasian' in Ball *et al*'s study (2000:37). However, the young Asian men did express a degree of fatalism in terms of their future domestic arrangements. Whilst Amir, who wanted to 'be a computer programmer', described a possible transition which would lead to 'a good job that I will stick with', he anticipated that once he had achieved this, he would 'get married, and live in a bigger town, not boring Townsville'. Amir's expectations also included a transition and employment before an arranged marriage, but for Samir, facing the added difficulty of physical disability, the prospect of employment was almost secondary:

> We tried to get me married off but it hasn't worked yet. [I will probably have] a job – I would like to work in an office answering phones, messages for anybody, working on computer ... bringing up a good family that can look after me, go to Pakistan.

For Samir, being 'looked after' by a future wife and family figured highly in his hopes for the future.

For all the young people in this group, the lifestyle ambitions they expressed were incongruous with their occupational aspirations. Indeed, rather than imagined futures, their lifestyle aspirations might better be described as fantasy futures. These fantasies included living in mansions, living abroad in exotic (and slightly less exotic) locations, apparently unlimited material wealth and (for the male students) the admiration and attention of many young women. This celebrity lifestyle, whilst unattainable for these young people, is one to which they are heavily exposed through the media, particularly through coverage of individual sports and popular music personalities such as David and Victoria Beckham, as well as through reality TV programmes such as *Big Brother* or *The X Factor*, in which they see people like themselves apparently achieving instant fame and affluence.

Although none of the occupational ambitions they expressed would support such a lifestyle, most would provide a regular income at national average levels or above and might be described as 'working class career jobs' (Ashton and Field, 1976 cited Hodkinson *et al*, 1996:7). However, for this group of young people such ambitions may be as unattainable as the fantasy lifestyle.

None of these young people had a clear idea of the credentials or education or work related routes necessary to access their chosen occupation. Al, for example, wanted 'high standard' qualifications in programming or engineering. He believed that this would take 'at least a few years' but was unsure how long or what type of qualification he needed. Likewise, Amir said 'I think I will [need higher level qualifications]' but was also unclear about the nature of those qualifications, or how long it might take to achieve them.

Choosing a 'good' qualification

Most of the IT students had arrived on the course by serendipity, rather than as part of a planned transition. Wayne had spent the previous year on another course at the same college 'I went to East Building close to North Building in Townsville and I did a Key Skills Building Year or something'. Pete had also progressed from other programmes 'Well, I was in college the past two years doing Next Step (pre level 1 programme) and engineering just to boost my grades up'. Emma had also progressed from 'another course'. She had wanted to do leisure and tourism but the programme failed to recruit and she was offered a place to do IT. Emma did not really know what course she had completed, or what credentials she had gained. She thought she might have two GCSEs, but could not remember either grades or subjects. Wayne was equally vague regarding his GCSE grades – he thought he had 'got a pass in every one' but '*I don't know whether I did good or bad* but I think I got a pass in every one' (my emphasis). Other students were similarly vague about their existing credentials. Al said that he had done a GNVQ in Applied IT and thought he had gained a 'high grade' though he was not specific about this. He had done this and 'the engineering course' after achieving what he described as 'poor' GCSE grades. He and Pete clarified this as 'Es and Fs really'.

Despite the almost accidental nature of their transitions, the students regarded the programme as a route to a 'good' qualification both in its own right and as a pathway to higher level credentials. Al believed the programme was about 'starting at the bottom, working your way up and get the best qualification in IT' and Samir that: 'You'll probably get a very good qualification if you can turn up at a certain time and in a certain place that you need to be in then you will get a very good qualification' . Similarly, Pete said that: 'Grandad says 'you will go far if you have some great qualifications behind you''.

In stark contrast to the optimism expressed by the students, the teaching team regarded the qualification as having little economic value and Nick suggested that the real value of the foundation award was as an educational stepping stone:

> They're not [likely to gain employment as a result of holding a level 1 credential] if you think the job they're gonna get from having a foundation or not having a foundation is not that different but I mean we've got kids now on National Diploma, on Level 3 who started with us on foundation, so we've got kids on HNDs who started on intermediate so it's giving them a bit of confidence and not everything can be judged on figures. Nick (Programme Co-ordinator, Foundation GNVQ IT)

This is consistent with Bathmaker's (2001) finding that level 1 programmes were considered to hold little credence outside the college but were valued as a progression route to level 2 programmes.

Hanging in

Of the eight students who participated in this study, five were successful in achieving a GNVQ foundation award. One (Emma) withdrew and a second (Naz) completed the course but failed to achieve the qualification. Samir was taking only part of the course as infill from the Special Needs programme he was enrolled on (see figure 4).

Name	Final Grade/Outcome	Destination
Samir	Infill – no grade	Foundation GNVQ IT
Wayne	Pass	Unknown
Al	Merit	DIDA
Pete	Pass	DIDA
Naz	Unclassified	Not Known
Amir	Pass	DIDA
Abdul	Pass	DIDA
Emma	Withdrawn	Not known

Figure 4: GNVQ IT students' destinations

Four students (Abdul, Amir, Pete and Al) all intended to progress to the Diploma in Digital Applications (DIDA), a new level 2 programme in IT. The college had no record as to the destination of either Naz or Emma, but neither had the skills or credentials necessary to work in their chosen occupation and it is possible that they have continued to work in the low pay, low skill occupations they were employed in whilst they were enrolled on the GNVQ programme. For Emma, this was work as a cleaner and for Naz, labouring for his father. Wayne did achieve his award, but left at the end of the year, again leaving no indication of his future destination. With a notion of the role of a salesman apparently rooted in the mid-twentieth century, his occupational ambition also seems likely to remain unfulfilled. Samir, who had done part of the programme without assessment as a broader special needs provision, intended to progress to the foundation programme, repeating the year with assessment.

Neil (tutor) talked at length about the nature of the personal difficulties some of the students brought with them. He ascribed much of the drop out as being due to these pressures, and felt that his own life experiences had given him particular empathy with such students:

> I think some don't pass this course for reasons outside colleges [control] ... there's nothing we can do about it they have problems at home and they go missing. You know, not missing from home – they just don't turn up to college and their own personal life sort of affects whether they pass or not. It's not through the lack of trying I think, because they are going through 16-18 year olds and all the hormones and the personal life and other pressures. I think that affects it and then you get the ones who just ... they just sort of disappear you just don't see them and they could be doing whatever, what they've got to do to survive I guess. Whether they've been kicked out, whether they've got their own place or whether there are other things they've got to deal with in life which I can relate to because I left home at 19 ... you know, you've got to get every student to pass but there are things beyond our control that you just can't ... you just can't plan for; you can't do anything about. Neil, (GNVQ foundation IT Tutor, St. Dunstan's)

Interview data supported Neil's view that many of the students had complex lives. Samir, for example, was struggling with obvious pressures associated with his disability as well as other exclusionary characteristics, and Pete had casually described finding his mother after she died from a drug overdose. Despite Neil's insight into these complex lives, he agreed with Nick that the real value of the award was the opportunity it provided to work towards level 2, the government's minimum for employability. This view suggests that these tutors had bought in to the government rhetoric of the learning society, in which ever higher levels of credential are necessary to succeed in the labour market (Bathmaker, 2005). However, although she subscribed to the belief that level 1 programmes provided an opportunity to progress to level 2, Sara, another tutor, had some particularly strong feelings about the programme, which she felt failed to meet students' expectations. She believed that students expected practical activities (such as surfing the net and producing power point presentations) and were unaware that IT programmes at all levels have a high business studies and management content. This was confirmed by Abdul who said that he 'like[d] doing presentations – they are exciting. We have finished all the boring stuff now'.

College: a better education?

The achievement of qualifications was not the only value the students placed on the programme. Naz said that 'It's about being treated with respect and no uniform' and Pete, who had struggled at school, valued the support he received from the tutors:

> I love it me, I think it's brilliant. I like how the lessons are handled because they explain better, they actually run over it different ways what you actually have to do on the course so it's more easier to understand.

This acknowledgement of the need for support, which is at variance with the students' perception of themselves as adults, was also evident in some of the presentations (see figure 5):

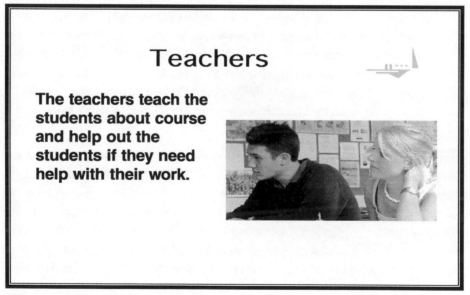

Figure 5: Slide 6/20 Pete and Al's presentation (serendipitous data)

The students' perceptions of college were that it was better than going to school, and there was a general perception amongst the students, evident in their interview data, that they were working hard. However, other data arising from the classroom observation and interviews with staff, as well as the students' own presentations, indicated that other things may be happening here, and that attending college formed an extension of their leisure activity. This was evident in discussions they had in the classroom during lessons when much of the chat was focussed on the discussion of various leisure activities with friends in the group.

Being able (or allowed) to talk was important to them. Wayne preferred college because 'Teachers let you have free time to talk to each other if you do your work so it's not like school' and Samir agreed saying that 'It is better than school – you can talk and work at the same time'.

In the classroom they were keen to show off the work they were doing, but also chatted at length amongst themselves, and most of the focus of this was around their leisure activities. Pete talked at length about his new boots, as well as about how much he had drunk the previous night, whilst Samir's conversation ranged from questions about what other people were doing, to what they might do at lunch time, to the music and other things he had found on the internet during the session. Pete and Al also succeeded in including leisure activity in an assessed presentation they produced about the GNVQ programme (figure 6).

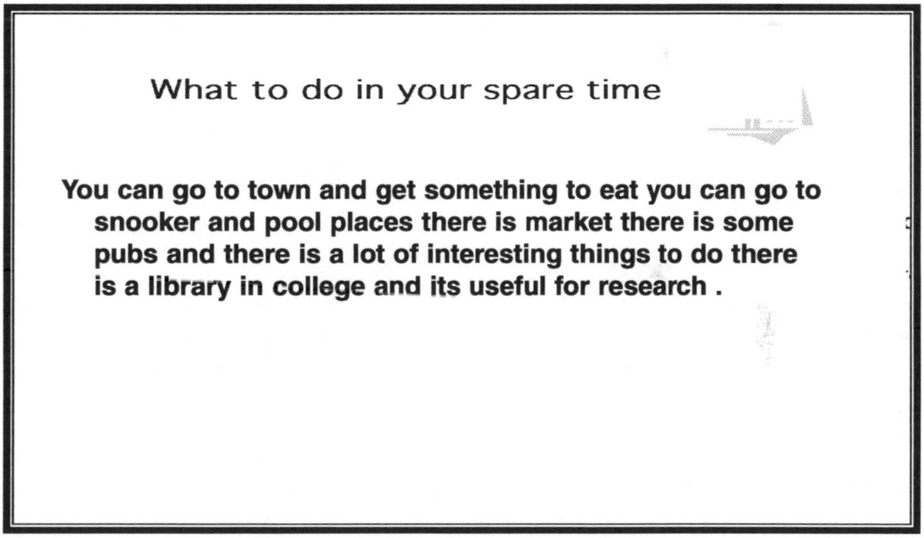

What to do in your spare time

You can go to town and get something to eat you can go to snooker and pool places there is market there is some pubs and there is a lot of interesting things to do there is a library in college and its useful for research .

Figure 6: Slide 7/20 Pete and Al's presentation (serendipitous data)

The perception that students' had of college as being 'better than school' and being 'treated with respect' seemed to be related to the approach taken by the staff team. Although the team was predominantly male (Nick and Neil did most of the teaching with a more limited commitment from Sara), there was evidence to suggest that the approach to teaching and pastoral care was nurturing and that it emphasised the vulnerability and support needs of the students. Neil described the importance of being 'really welcoming' and discussed the 'issues' he believed the young people had and their need for support. He regarded college as a better option than work for them because 'you can't take your personal issues and baggage into work' and considered that level 1 students needed 'a longer timescale' to make the transition from 'school kids to adults'.

Similarly to Neil, and also using a discourse of fragility, Nick talked of half the group having 'social and emotional difficulties' saying that 'quite a few of them have got sort of baggage and things like that, that they do bring with them like emotional wise' and describing them as 'low in confidence ... really'. He also subscribed to the notion that level 1 students were more in need of support than those at higher levels, attributing a level of blame and responsibility to intermediate students:

> I find the difference between foundation and intermediate kids [is that] a lot of the time the foundation kids if you give them a bit of encouragement they will listen to you more and if you do have to tell them off they will sort of be quiet and pay attention. Whereas intermediate kids tend to be a bit brighter but tend not to do as well as they should have done, through – probably more through their own fault more than the foundations, so they tend to be the harder ones to control I find. Nick (Programme Co-ordinator, GNVQ IT Foundation)

Support from staff, and relationships with them, had been given a high profile in the students' interviews. These relationships were a significant factor in the students' overtly positive attitude to learning. The positive personal rhetoric was, however, in tension with other data. All except Emma had enthused about the course and expressed a commitment to attend and get a good qualification. Wayne, for example, conflated good attendance with achievement and said that 'I'm attending every day. I've probably missed one or two days in the whole of the time I've been here'. However, Nick's assessment of Wayne's attendance was 'poor'. The students' perception was that they were working hard, and this was reflected in their keenness to share with me the presentations they were working on. This dichotomy between the students' belief that they were working 'hard' and other available evidence was also noted by Bathmaker (2005) and is explored further in section 3.

The tendency for students to regard their learning programme as part of a wider leisure activity was also highlighted by Neil who said that:

For these [students] I think it [the social aspects of the programme] holds a[s] big a social value, ...I'm probably going to get slated for this but I think it's as this is as big a social event as a learning event, because they get to meet friends and I've seen students sort of grow up and sort of learn how to socialise ... sometimes they go off the rails and go to pubs, and are arguing and things but that's all part of growing up I suppose. I think it's a big social thing. Neil (Tutor, Foundation GNVQ IT)

Having fun, hanging around

For the IT group, the most important thing in life was leisure and 'having fun'. Many of the group used the term 'hanging around with friends' to describe their activities. For this predominantly male group, the key activities they engaged in during leisure time were sport, computer or alcohol related, and this was common across both the cultural groups represented. However, whilst those students from the local white ethnic community engaged in these activities with friends, those from the Pakistani ethnic community engaged in such activities with both friends and their extended family, usually relatives described as cousins.

Wayne, who enjoyed fishing at a competitive level, had recently won £500 and another trophy to add to his collection of silver cups. He was exceptional in this, however, in that no other student participated in a leisure activity which held the possibility of financial reward. Therefore, for Wayne and for other students, most leisure activity was funded by part time employment or benefits (see figure 7).

Student	Existing Financial support/employment
Samir	Benefits
Wayne	P/T Shop Assistant
Al	P/T Kitchen Porter/EMA
Pete	Child Benefit
Naz	P/T Labourer
Amir	P/T Shop assistant
Abdul	Parental support
Emma	F/T Cleaner

Figure 7: Sources of financial support for GNVQ IT students

Only one student (Abdul) reported being exclusively dependent on his parents, and whilst none of the types of employment the students engaged in might be described as anything more than low skill, low pay work, some falling within the casualised, informal economy, their employment did provide these young people with a tenuous hold on the world of work and the possibility of future employment. Naz and Amir both worked with their fathers, a familial link which could prove useful in the future. Emma's job as a cleaner was both full time and permanent and Al, whilst at the time of interview working as a kitchen porter on a casual basis, was awaiting an interview for a job as a checkout operator at his local Tesco store.

The importance of money and its relationship to leisure was highlighted by Wayne, who described his part time job in a local shop for cash in hand as 'just a little job to get me money for the weekend so I can do what I like, a few sports, have a drink, whatever'. Samir, Al, Pete, Naz and Amir all highlighted 'hanging around with friends' as an important part of their leisure activity and most of the group identified group activities as being fundamental to their leisure time. Hanging around meant being with other young people, accepted as part of that group and engaged in conversation with them. This did not necessarily need to be associated with any other activity, and was regarded by them as having significance in its own right.

Many of the group activities these young people engaged in were sports related – football, rugby, cricket and basketball all figured highly. Others were related to the consumption of alcohol and their comments suggested that these young people, despite most being under 18, and irrespective of ethnicity or religion, were engaged in a heavy drinking culture. Both Naz and Amir identified 'going for a drink' as important, whereas others participated in activities which might involve the use of alcohol. Abdul, for example, spent time regularly at his local snooker hall with his friends. Other evidence of students engaging with a drinking culture was provided by their presentations and discussions during class activities. Pete, who talked about participating in a range of apparently innocuous and often solitary activities: 'Play on the play-station, go on computer. Sometimes I go swimming or go out with my mates – half the time I am with my mates. I enjoy rock music and sci-fi space programmes. I collect Warhammer' discussed his heavy drinking at length in class and produced a presentation on 'My favourite food' which consisted of a series of slides listing a vast range of alcoholic drinks.

Samir, whose leisure, like his education, was constrained by his physical limitations, spent much of his leisure time engaged in solitary activities but looked forward to Saturdays:

> For me, me and my mates meet up. We sometimes go [to the pub] for a drink, we all like the same. We sometimes go to McDonalds; we have a really good time. At home I play on play station or watch telly. A lot of time is spent playing on the play station or watching telly but on Saturday I meet up with my mates and have a good time. I do whatever they do. I *really* do whatever they do. (original emphasis) (Samir, IT)

Samir demonstrated more characteristics associated with social exclusion than any other member of this group (special education, lack of credentials, ethnicity, disability, poverty and social class), perhaps placing him at the bottom of a societal stratification which constitutes layers of inclusion and not just a distinction between inclusion and exclusion (Bathmaker, 2005). His final, reiterated sentence reflected a quiet desperation – an attempt to keep 'hanging in' through participation in leisure as much as in education and find a place in society which would allow him to be included, rather than excluded.

Summary

This group of young people enjoyed attending college and had high hopes for their future in a digital world. These hopes had a dreamlike quality. The students imagined the affluence associated with some parts of the IT industry, and a celebrity lifestyle that they hoped such an income could sustain. They believed that the 'good' qualification they would achieve – a GNVQ Foundation IT award – would provide the basis for such a career. Knowledge about career pathways, credentials and the potential length of transition was limited to Abdul who had observed closely his cousins' transitions through higher education.

However, despite an expressed commitment to learning and achieving credentials (and the interest, commitment and nurturing of the staff team) three of the eight students who participated in the study left education and only one of these achieved the foundation award. Four -only half the group – progressed to level 2, with Samir remaining at college to complete the foundation award over a second year.

The expressed commitment to learning conflicted with the more primary importance of leisure activity in the lives of the young people. It was also apparent that the effort the young people invested in leisure, in terms of both the leisure activity itself and in acquiring the money to finance it, far outweighed the investment they made in learning. However, they seemed unaware of this and all believed they were 'working hard' – and they saw no dissonance between their investment in leisure and their visions of an affluent digital future.

the young people all said that their parents worked in occupations which might be described as low pay, low skill work and none of their parents, siblings or extended family members had pursued education beyond level 2, the equivalent to GCSE (see figure 8).

Eight of thirteen mothers were known to be in employment although three students (Kelly, Jennifer and Brady) did not know what their mother's occupation was. Where occupation was known, it followed strong gender divisions, reflecting traditional roles in the local community. Two mothers were employed as cleaners, one as a shop assistant and one as a care assistant. One mother worked in a food processing factory but the nature of her job role was unclear to her daughter (Paris). Cameron's mother was an unpaid carer. As well as having strongly gendered occupational backgrounds, three of the parents of students in this group were reported as disabled and a further three were working as paid or unpaid carers, possible influences on their daughters, who had enrolled on a HSC programme. Another parent was employed as an unpaid charity fundraiser, a giving and altruistic occupation which might also be seen to have an – albeit nebulous – link with caring.

Of those siblings whose gender was reported, most were female (16 out of 21). Although the gender of all siblings was not reported (two students had unspecified 'brothers and sisters'), the focus of most students' responses was on female rather than male siblings. The exception to this was Jade who wrote that 'I love looking after my special needs little brother'. However, whilst her comment referred to a brother, its emphasis appeared to be less on gender and more on caring and domesticity. This focus on gender and caring is interesting given the marked gender divisions in the programme the group were enrolled on, and the fact that they were drawn from a working class community which still adheres to very traditional gender roles in which caring is located as a female activity associated with responsibility and respectability (Skeggs, 1997:54).

Eleven of the twelve students interviewed aspired to gender stereotypical, caring jobs (see figure 9). Seven wanted to work in childcare and two as a nurse or midwife. Naomi hoped to become a social worker and Jade, influenced by her experience with her 'special needs little brother' wanted to be a special needs teacher. The exception was Keira. Already the sole full time carer for a terminally ill mother, she could see no future beyond fulfilling this role and had no plans for any future occupation.

Student	Mother	Father	Siblings
Paris	Factory worker	Fundraiser (unpaid)	1. Unknown
Jennifer	'Mum works everywhere'	Shelf stacking	1. Sister – Mecca Bingo Hall 2. Sister – Mecca Bingo Hall 3. Brother – Army
Keira	Disabled	No contact	No siblings
Brady	Not known	Fork lift truck driver – supervisory role	1. Sister – Cleaner 2. Brother in law – shop assistant
Kate	Unemployed	Unemployed	Older siblings, gender not reported 1. Sister – McDonalds others not known
Angelina	Housewife	Builder	1. Sister – Schoolchild
Jade	Cleaner	Care Assistant	1. Brother – Working 2. Brother- Schoolchild with special needs 3. Sister – Schoolchild
Alice	Care Assistant	Disabled	1. Sister – Non-working mother 2. Sister – Non-working mother 3. Sister – Non-working mother 4. 5 Younger siblings, gender not reported
Rea	Cleaner	P/T Computer Repairs	1. Sister – Schoolchild 2. Sister – Schoolchild
Britney	Shop Worker	Postman & Doorman	1. Sister – Shop Assistant (Jewellers) 2. Sister – Shop Assistant (Boots) 3. Sister – schoolchild
Cameron	Cares for dad	'Ill'	1. Sister – Asda 2. Brother- Schoolchild 3. Brother – Schoolchild
Kelly	Working	Working	1. Sister – Schoolchild
Rukhsana	Not Interviewed	Not interviewed	Not interviewed

Figure 8: Occupational and educational backgrounds of HSC students' parents and siblings

Imagined futures

The young people were asked what they hoped they would be doing in five or ten years' time, when they had finished their education. In order to establish whether they had any role models, they were also asked whether they knew anyone who was already employed in the same role. Only two of the group could be said to have a role model of any description (see figure 9). Rea, who hoped to pursue a career in childcare, had previously worked at Wacky Warehouse, a national chain of indoor adventure play areas for small children, where other staff who held recognised childcare qualifications had encouraged her ambitions. Alice hoped to be a nurse and, whilst she did not know anyone already working as a nurse, her mother was a care assistant in a nursing home, providing a possible link to potential role models.

There were some tensions between the occupational aspirations of the group and the lifestyle aspirations that some of them expressed. Where lifestyle aspirations were included, they all involved an expectation of future wealth and affluence which was not consistent with the type of occupation they aspired to. For Paris, her lifestyle aspirations included 'a mansion in North Yorkshire, a Porsche' . Brady and Naomi both hoped to 'own my own house in London' and Kate, who had never travelled overseas, hoped to be working abroad.

This preoccupation with a wealthy lifestyle extended to the students' leisure activity in terms of their interest in popular culture and the lifestyle of celebrities such as the Beckhams. The group also watched a range of popular competitive television programmes in which the winner received significant cash rewards and/or instant fame such as *Big Brother, X Factor, Who wants to be a millionaire?* and *I'm a celebrity get me out of here*. This was strongly reflected in their pseudonyms for this book. The young people all chose their own pseudonyms and all were taken from celebrities – well known characters in television programmes, pop stars, models or Hollywood actresses.

This group had superficially pragmatic, if gendered, career related expectations (see figure 9); for example, Alice wanted to 'go to university and be a nurse'; Jade to 'be a teacher' and Rea to 'go to university'. However, only two had the benefit of a mentor or role model to support them to achieve their career aim and there was a further dissonance between these ambitions and the students' other ideas for the future. Both Rea and Alice, whilst talking at length about their plans to go to university and prepare for professional roles, indicated that they might leave college at the end of their level 1 course to 'get some money behind me'.

Student	Occupational Aspiration	Do you know anyone doing this job now?
Paris	Midwifery, then to teach midwifery	No
Jennifer	Nursery Nursing, then to teach Nursery Nursing	No
Keira	No aspiration	No
Brady	Nursery Nursing, then to teach Nursery Nursing	Yes
Kate	Catering or working in a Nursery	Catering – sister works at McDonalds
Angelina	Nursery Nurse	N/A
Jade	Special Needs Teacher	No, but younger sibling has special needs
Alice	Nursing	Mother a Care Assistant
Rea	Childcare	Yes – I used to work at Wacky Warehouse
Britney	Childcare (secure job)	Not childcare – sisters in 'secure jobs'
Cameron	Childcare	No
Naomi	Social Work	No
Rukhsana	Not Interviewed	Not Interviewed

Figure 9: Students' occupational aspirations and potential role models

Early in the year all these young women suggested that they had bought into credentialism as a route to success and expressed commitment to obtaining 'good' jobs requiring 'qualifications'. Despite this, none of the group had any notion of the career path or credentials they would need to pursue to achieve their ambitions and, like the young people in Bathmaker's (2001) study, they showed no inclination to investigate this. Jade, who said that she wanted to be a special needs teacher, was typical of this:

Liz	So, Jade, you want to be a special needs teacher. Do you know how long it will take you to get there?
Jade	Roughly about three to four years.
Liz	And what would you have to do to become a special needs teacher?
Jade	Erm ... a course on childcare probably, and something higher up the special needs thing.
Liz	Would you need to go to university or anything like that?
Jade	I don't think so.

Kate's response was equally if not more confused:

Liz	What sort of job with children would you like?
Kate	Class Assistant, a nanny something like that.
Liz	Do you know what sort of qualifications you need for that?
Kate	Yes.
Liz	What do you need?
Kate	I can't remember.

Despite this, she was confident that in the future, she would have a 'secure job' working with children.

Although they were unclear about possible pathways, the students regarded their course as a route to other programmes which would eventually enable them to fulfil their hopes and aspirations. This notion of low level vocational courses as a pathway was also apparent in the staff interviews which focused on the Foundation HSC award as a route to other programmes and then to specific occupations. John, the Programme Co-ordinator, considered that the programme:

...certainly prepares those who are capable for a higher level of education which is very good [and as well as progressing to level 2] some students have actually gone on and gone to work in residential care homes, nursing homes and have actually gone onto the NVQ route after obtaining that level, but obviously their practical skills have to be achieved as well.

Later, placing his faith in the new partnership agreement between St. Dunstan's and a local NHS trust, he suggested that:

They may not achieve their aspirations of being fully registered staff within that sphere of employment. They may well obtain a lower level of employment within that and they have some background skills as well which could be utilised.

This comment suggests that low level vocational programmes such as the GNVQ are effectively preparing students for lower level caring jobs as a substitute for their original ambitions to be nurses and teachers. However, for most of this group, who aspired to work with children, caring jobs within the local NHS trust would be unlikely to involve caring for children, and would be more likely to involve caring for the elderly, disabled or other vulnerable groups.

Sue, a subject tutor on the programme, also viewed the programme as a pathway to higher level programmes: 'I think they are preparing for a job [but] I think they need another course of study'. Jim, the classroom support assistant, took a more critical view. He believed that the foundation GNVQ did provide a qualification but also that it 'massages the unemployment figures'. He had strong views about the programme as a whole and considered vocational Further Education programmes to be no different to the secondary modern education available in his youth when 'you had A, B, C and D streams. A did science and D did gardening'. Within this framework, vocational education in Further Education was clearly related to secondary modern education, and level 1 programmes – the lowest level of vocational education – to the gardening D stream.

Choosing a 'good' qualification

The students on the HSC programme all believed that they had 'chosen' their course and regarded it as a route to the career of their choice. However, they had all chosen the subject but not the level of their programme and were unaware of the implications of beginning a course of study at level 1 or of the lack of credibility of such credentials. Angelina had chosen the programme 'So we could get some more experience so I can go into childcare' and this was endorsed by Jade, Paris and Brady who had come on the programme for similar reasons. Cameron was the only student to mention credentials, and discussed her lack of qualifications, rather than the relative worth of the GNVQ. She said that 'I did it because I'm working my way up to actually working with children. I started here because I didn't get very good grades at school'. Other students qualified their reasons for choosing the programme with statements such as 'doing my qualifications' (Jade) and 'because I didn't get right good [grades] in my GCSEs' (Alice).

Such statements seemed to reflect a commitment to continuing to study although other data, discussed later, conflicted with this. However, these views could be attributed to the young people echoing the lifelong learning rhetoric they hear from the teaching staff and the institution, which in turn are influenced by government rhetoric and policy, and by local and media interpretations of these.

Amongst the staff, both Sue and John considered that the Educational Maintenance Allowance (EMA), which provides a means tested allowance for 16-19 year olds in full time education and training dependent on attendance and engagement with the programme, was an important factor in individual students' decisions to enrol on the programme. However, Sue also believed that 'Some of them maybe want another chance because they have not achieved at school'. However, whilst many of the students regarded college as an opportunity to gain credentials and achieve their hopes and ambitions, none of them gave financial reasons for *coming* to college – none reported enrolling on a programme in order to claim EMA for example – although some suggested that financial difficulties might lead them to *leave* college in order to find full time employment.

A number of students said that parental support was a factor which influenced their decision to come to college. In all but one case, this was associated with parents' aspirations for their offspring to achieve 'good' qualifications and 'good' jobs. However, the Foundation GNVQ is not recognised as an acceptable credential in the Care industry, a situation which also applies to its successor qualifications, the Specialised Diploma and BTEC Introductory Certificate. Government regulation stipulates that the minimum qualification to work in Care is an NVQ level 2. Employment within the sector is also limited to over eighteens, so for these students, aged 17 at the end of their programme, the only option within their chosen field was to progress to the BTEC First Diploma in Care/Health for which the minimum entry requirement was a Merit at Foundation level. In fact, only five of the thirteen students were expected to achieve this by the end of the programme and two others were borderline pass/merit (see figure 10). This was a source of some concern to John:

> The concern that I have is with the basic pass grade students where they go from there, because quite often I just get the feeling that there is the possibility they may just get lost and go out into employment. John (Programme Co-ordinator GNVQ Foundation HSC)

A simple analysis of the progression data for this group as shown in figure 10 illustrates the probable accuracy of John's comments.

Six students were expecting to achieve a pass. Of these, five gave their planned destination as 'undecided'. One expected to move to a different voca-

Student	Final Predicted Grade	Planned Destination
Paris	Unclassified	Employment
Jennifer	Merit	BTEC First Diploma – Health
Keira	Pass	Undecided
Brady	Merit	Leaving Destination unknown
Kate	Pass	Catering
Angelina	Distinction	BTEC First Diploma – Health
Jade	Pass	Undecided
Alice	Pass/Merit	Undecided
Rea	Pass	Undecided
Britney	Distinction	BTEC First Diploma – Health
Cameron	Distinction	Cache Certificate (Child care)
Kelly	Pass/Merit	Undecided
Rukhsana	Unclassified	Leaving Destination Unknown

Figure 10: Predicted grades and planned destinations HSC GNVQ Foundation

tional area with lower entry requirements at level 2. The option for the other four is to do the same, or to seek unskilled employment. Five achieved Merit or above, and of these, four intended to progress to level 2 programmes. One intended to leave, destination unknown. Two were unclassified and of these Paris intended to take up full time work outside the care sector, whilst Rukhsana had no plans for the future.

Hanging in

The group as a whole bought in to the credentialist society and lifelong learning, and part of this was their perception, individually and as a group, that they were 'working hard'. Angelina had given up a Saturday job, ostensibly to concentrate on course work:

I did have a Saturday job but it didn't go that well, I used to have a Saturday job but it didn't work out, because you haven't got time for studying. *It didn't work that well because when I went to college at first I used to get tired and that with all the work.* (My emphasis) Angelina (HSC)

Paris and Brady also highlighted this tension between work and college:

Paris	[I work] and it's really hard especially when you're 16. You are there, well I'm there every single day until Friday and that's my last day, good Friday. And I work five hours every day, non-stop. It gets to you sometimes. You feel like it's hard work, you're choosing college or work or...
Brady	Not going with your mates
Paris	It's so you're like "I wanna go and see my mates" but you can't because you are in work or you're in college. I still see my friends in college because I'm with them every day but if I want to spend some time with them at night, I can't because I'm working. So I find it hard.

It was clear that the group perceived time in college in similar terms to the way they perceived time at work – as a necessary occupation which prevented them from participating in the leisure activities they enjoyed. They all emphasised the amount of time they spent in college, despite the fact that all full time Further Education courses are currently delivered over only sixteen hours, or three working days. Although Paris clearly differentiated between seeing her friends at college and seeing them in the evening, she regarded both as forms of social activity and saw no conflict between this, the overt educational purpose of her college course and the fact that she had expressed a commitment to continue learning and pursuing a career in midwifery. However, the demands of attending the programme for sixteen hours a week, together with the 25 hours she worked, must have been significant and she was far from unique in having to work alongside her college course.

Financial difficulties were highlighted by the young people as being a key pressure. There were two, very different, reasons for these difficulties. Some members of the group had to contribute to the family income but all discussed a need to finance (often expensive) leisure activities. Paris worked because her mother insisted that she support herself and Alice had to contribute to her family's income because her mother was 'on the minimum wage'. Financial pressures created other difficulties for Alice as well: her domestic responsibilities arose largely from the fact that her mother worked twelve to fourteen hours at a stretch to maximise the family income and, as the eldest daughter, she was expected to fulfil her mother's domestic role in her absence.

Domesticity

Whilst not forming part of their imagined futures, family, home and domesticity were key features of life for five of the young women in the HSC group and significant in the lives of others. Kate and Keira both cared for a disabled mother, Rukhsana for younger siblings and Alice had a disabled parent – a father with diabetes and an associated heart complaint – and cared for five younger siblings whilst her mother worked. Jade cared for a younger brother who had 'special needs'.

Domesticity was a key feature in the way the young women in this group described themselves – for example, seven members of the group mentioned relationships with close family members ('I like helping my mum'). Jennifer, Jade, Cameron and Naomi all liked children and/or babysitting. Brady described herself as 'kind to children, kind and friendly' whilst Angelina said about herself 'I am kind, caring, polite, good manners. I like children', all suggesting the development of a caring 'self' (Skeggs, 1997:56).

However, there was a tension between the HSC students' caring identities, reflected in their choice of programme and in their individual caring roles, and in their expressed rejection of fulfilling 'wife and mother' female roles. Only three of thirteen students (Brady, Paris and Jennifer) included children in their imagined future and of these only Jennifer thought that a partner might form part of this future. Even she expressed pessimism about this, or possibly about the nature of any future relationship:

Jennifer	I'd like a proper boyfriend to do it for me
Liz	What's a proper boyfriend?
Jennifer	Somebody that won't hurt you, somebody who won't push you int't ground

None of the three young women who talked about the possibility of having children had caring responsibilities, so their view of motherhood may have been somewhat rose tinted. The impact of marriage and domesticity on older sisters was a factor in the rejection of that option by other members of the HSC group. Kate's facial expression and tone of voice (see emphasis) communicated her negativity far more effectively than her words during the following exchange:

Liz	Did any of them [siblings] go to college or ...
Kate	My sister Kim did
Liz	Do you know what she did?
Kate	I think she were doing the same as me, she wanted to work with children until she got pregnant
Liz	And now she's got her own?
Kate	*Yeah. Three of them* (Kate's own emphasis)

Alice also placed a low value on the role of mother as opposed to gaining credentials:

> My mum's wanting me to be ... go into a job where it's qualified and there's plenty of money behind it 'cos she wants me to do good. Like my sisters, I've got three sisters older than me and they've turned out to be just mums. They've got nowhere in college and nowt like that and I just want to prove to me mum that I want ... I can do it and get far. Alice (HSC)

Alice's comments were ambivalent. Her rejection of motherhood and domesticity was consistent with her apparent 'buy in' to credentialism and lifelong learning, which she expressed as a hope that she would 'go to university and be a nurse'. Despite being so clear about her plans for the future, at the end of the programme she thought that she might leave college to 'get some money behind me' before returning to education at a later, unspecified, date.

College: a better education

The importance of college to the HSC group focussed around two things – one being leisure and social activity, and the second being a perception of being valued. The perception of being valued, as with the IT group, appeared to be related to the relationships with and nurturing by the staff team. Angelina and Jade enjoyed 'doing work and project work' and felt the course was 'a lot better than school'. However, they placed the greatest value on the fact that 'You get treated more like adults and things like that'. Jennifer felt that the tutors were more like friends than teachers: 'Right, I think it's tutors me, tutors give you a lot of help a lot of guidance so they're your friends what are in college, your new friends what you've made in college'.

Staff also commented on, and ascribed great importance to, the relationships with students as part of the overall pastoral care for the group. Sue (HSC Tutor), an ex-nurse, described her own approach to the group, explaining that it exemplified the way she tried to make them feel valued:

> I think I need to know them as people, and they bring an awful lot of their issues and problems with them and I need to be aware of that, sharing a lot, they come in and they are talking about clothes and what they bought somebody and they are showing me. I think I have to show an interest in that before I can move on with a lesson ... Naomi does dancing, and sort of what they've done, what's on television, even the work when they are cutting and sticking bits in I'll have a look, because they want to share that with me, and I am pleased to help. Sue (HSC Tutor)

Whilst Sue's comments were intended to illustrate the way in which she demonstrated value for her students, they also illustrated the discourse of vulnerability which was used by the staff team, and were also illuminating in terms of demonstrating the type of discussion that students participate in during class time. These activities primarily related to leisure and social activity (talking about clothes, what they bought, dancing, what is on television) rather than learning activity (cutting and sticking). John, the course leader and also an ex-nurse, took a similar approach. He believed that nurturing relationships which demonstrated respect for the students helped them to develop respect for others:

> It (foundation HSC) does teach interpersonal skills and that's not just dealing with each other and respecting each other and valuing each other's special gifts but also those of the tutors that they work with. It's a fairly informal structure unless something goes seriously wrong in the class and the students refer to us as by our first names for example, not Mr or Mrs and we try to impress on the students that they are now in adult education and try and treat them and ensure the students behave as such. John (Programme Co-ordinator Foundation GNVQ HSC)

This was an important point as much of the activity the students engaged in during class time involved 'socialising', inherent in which was the rehearsal of interpersonal skills such as the use of mobile phones, sharing of treats such as sweets, and an episode when Rea was comforted by her friends after she became distressed by a dispute between Kate and Jade.

The way the staff team responded to this sort of behaviour in the classroom also indicated a strong nurturing ethos, which could possibly be ascribed to their professional backgrounds. All members of the HSC teaching team had originally trained in the caring professions, most of them in nursing. As a nurse, Sue perceived and fulfilled an extra dimension to her pastoral role, in that she had begun to take responsibility for students' health issues: 'Certainly being a nurse, if they find a lump or bump I need to see it, and tell them they need to see someone else sometimes, sometimes just a little word and I'll calm them down'.

Similarly, John described the type of student issue he was required to deal with, although he emphasised 'social and emotional difficulties' rather than health issues, and did not provide health advice in the way his colleague did:

> In my experience we have had students who are the total carer for the family where the student has to deliver 24 hour care with very little support at home and then come into the college. Some students have part time jobs which obviously impinges [on college]. Some students have sexual health issues, we have some students who come from disruptive families with broken family backgrounds but they honestly do believe that they can achieve and I think that's the prime concern that they see ... something at the end of [the course] whether it's realistic or not is [debatable] I suppose. John (Programme Co-ordinator Foundation GNVQ HSC)

The students' own belief in their ability to achieve was also very apparent throughout the course of the study. They had no doubt that they would realise their ambitions. Members of the staff team were more cautious about achievement. John suggested that despite the young people's self belief, the social and emotional barriers he had described might well be insurmountable.

Having fun, hanging around

Whilst the students talked about being committed to learning and achieving credentials, other data suggested that social and leisure activity was more important to them than learning. This was particularly evident in the classroom when the students engaged in a multitude of activities mostly unrelated to any aspect of their learning programme during learning time. During a classroom observation, the whole group participated in writing a birthday card for a friend, whilst Keira gave out sweets and other students engaged in general discussion. Some of this was related to a texted conversation Alice was engaging in with a friend, and to the photograph her friend had sent her. At one point Alice telephoned Rea, who was sitting next to her. Kate was discussing an impending shopping trip to buy a top.

After my observation of the group, I asked them to complete a sheet showing a 5 scale point grid to identify how hard they felt they had worked during the session. This arose from my observation of them engaging in activity which was largely social rather than learning related. The results of this are shown in figure 11 – only one student acknowledged that she had been chatting to her friends and had not really worked very hard at all. Clearly, the students' perception of 'hard work' was very different to mine.

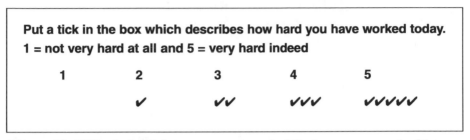

Put a tick in the box which describes how hard you have worked today.
1 = not very hard at all and 5 = very hard indeed

1	2	3	4	5
	✔	✔✔	✔✔✔	✔✔✔✔✔

Figure 11: HSC students' own assessment of their engagement with learning

In terms of the importance placed on learning activity, it is perhaps significant that when the students wrote individual profiles, describing themselves and their lives, only three mentioned liking college. However, all included social activity with friends as part of their profile. For example, 'I like ... going [out] with friends and my boyfriend'. (Jennifer); 'I like dancing, going out with friends' (Kate) and 'I like hanging around with friends, listening to music and going to the pictures' (Britney).

This type of engagement in social activity was evident in every aspect of the data for the group and learning appeared to be required to fit in to this imperative. The students who were more heavily engaged in domestic activity were largely locked into domesticity and denied the opportunity to develop alternative identities outside the female caring role. Alice, for example regarded her 'lifestyle' as 'different' to that of her friends and Keira had one evening a week respite from caring for her mother. She spent this at Jennifer's house, where she 'looked after' the small children of two of Jennifer's relatives. Other than caring for her mother, Keira's only aspiration for the future was 'to be (friends) with these three' (Paris, Jennifer and Brady).

Angelina and Jade, who had fewer domestic responsibilities, passed their leisure time in 'Swimming, going to the cinema, sports, hanging around with our mates, all stuff like that'. Asked to define 'hanging around' they described it as '...just socialising, going skating, catching up on gossip, stuff like that' whilst Kate, who 'hung around' with both her boyfriend and with her female friendship group described it as being '...like in town and something like that and walking around with some of my mates'.

Inevitably, many of these social and leisure activities potentially involved a significant financial cost. Whilst many of the activities the students engaged in had a cost attached to them (eg cinema, ice skating) Brady summed up the greatest leisure cost when she described her hobbies as 'Swimming, going to the cinema, shopping – it's my favourite thing, shopping'. She was not unusual in this – shopping was a key social activity for many of this group. However, only three students were employed and funded their leisure activities independently. Eight students received EMA and used this to fund their leisure activity. Three students (Rea, Britney and Cameron) did not receive EMA. They suggested that this was due to the complexities of claiming the benefit, rather than because their family income was above the EMA threshold. However, this meant that all three were dependent on their parents, who provided 'pocket money' to fund leisure and social activity (figure 12).

Student	Existing Financial Support
Paris	P/T Factory work
Jennifer	EMA
Keira	EMA
Brady	EMA
Kate	EMA and work on ice cream van
Angelina	EMA (had previously worked at newsagents)
Jade	EMA (had previously worked in clothes shop)
Alice	EMA and working at fish and chip shop
Rea	Dependent on parents (had previously worked at Wacky Warehouse).
Britney	Dependent on parents
Cameron	Dependent on parents
Naomi	EMA
Rukhsana	Not Interviewed

Figure 12: Sources of financial support for HSC students

Whilst expensive, the activities the group engaged in were undertaken for 'fun' and were largely unstructured. Only Naomi was engaged in a structured leisure activity, dancing, and to 'carry on with my dancing career' formed one of her options for future employment, one which, moreover, was supported by her parents who saw it as an alternative to HSC.

> My dad says that if I don't like you know succeed with this course then they'd like me to – you know do – I can't even say it – cho...[choreography] ... I done near enough all my exams I've got four or five more left for my teachers exams so... Naomi (HSC)

Although Naomi had the possibility of developing her leisure activity into something more concrete, for the others it was their source of pleasure and enjoyment in a world where they were struggling to achieve a credential which held minimal recognition, and were facing either an extended transition (which would affect their ability to finance their leisure activity, particularly once EMA was withdrawn at the age of 19) or a move into the drudgery of low pay, low skill employment. It is unsurprising that in these circumstances so much time and effort was invested in leisure, and so much importance attributed to it.

Summary

This group demonstrated many conflicts in their hopes and aspirations for the future. All reported high aspirations which could be divided into lifestyle and occupational aspirations. The lifestyle aspirations had a heavy celebrity influence, and were primarily hopes of sudden transformation which would result in celebrity status and, perhaps more importantly, the affluence associated with such status. Their occupational aspirations were high, with most hoping to move on to a skilled or professional role. The implication of those ambitions was that the minimum transition any student could expect was three years (for nursery nursing), and in some cases this rose to as much as seven years (for nursing, teaching and midwifery). However, none had any idea of the pathways and credentials necessary to achieve their aspirations, nor of the length of transition they could expect.

John, the programme co-ordinator, questioned how 'realistic' their aspirations were, suggesting that they may eventually find employment in low level caring roles rather than in the professional capacity they aspired to. In tension with this recognition of the likely reality for the young people, their self-belief and conviction that they could achieve their ambitions were nurtured within a caring ethos which placed a significant emphasis on social and emotional development.

The young people themselves expressed a commitment to attending college and getting a good education in order to achieve their ambitions, but also talked about leaving college to find employment and earn money. Further, despite an overt rejection of stereotypical female roles by most of the group, all were involved in rehearsing domesticity to a greater or lesser extent. Their course was intended to prepare them for a stereotypical female caring role and most were involved in caring and domestic activity in the home. The few who did not have significant responsibilities in the home did have dreams of a future with their own home and children. For this group, education was taking place in a context of conflicting and confused hopes and ambitions heavily influenced by social and familial constraints.

7

Serving time: Woodlands College level 1 group

Introduction

The Level 1 group at Woodlands College had originally applied for different courses, except for two students (Richard and Hamish) who both had statements of special educational need and had progressed to the programme from pre-level 1 provision in the College. Despite the best efforts of the teaching team, those young people who were categorised as mainstream students regarded the course as a form of serving time, in which their futures were on hold until they were able to move on to a different course which they perceived to be more relevant to their interests and aspirations.

Group profile

The level 1 group at Woodlands College consisted of eleven students. Five were male and six female and they came from varied ethnic backgrounds which were representative of the local community. Six of these students (Max, Leonardo, Catherine, Richard, Hamish and Mohammed) were interviewed, though the others contributed enthusiastically to other aspects of data collection. For this reason, all are included in this discussion. All the young people in the group had had difficult educational experiences which included permanent exclusion, special needs education and severe disruption associated with having refugee status. They were all enrolled on the level 1 programme, a new initiative by the college to try and address perceived weaknesses in the GNVQ foundation curriculum. It provided the opportunity to gain a range of small credentials and had a focus on basic literacy and numeracy. Literacy and numeracy credentials were available at Entry, level 1 and level 2, according to the level at which the student was working. Students also spent one day a week working towards NVQ level 1 units in a choice of four vocational areas. The specialist level 1 team included Janet, the Head of Department for Foundation Studies, and Pat, the Programme Manager. Four other tutors, Gabby, Paul, Will and Jaskaren also taught on the programme.

All the young people in the group came from areas of significant disadvantage. Where parental occupation was known to the students, they all described working class job roles except for Leonardo, whose mother was a counsellor. Like Richard and Hamish, Leonardo also had siblings who had participated in Higher Education.

Student	Mother	Father	Siblings
Max	Check out Manager at Tesco	Not Known	1. Home help
			2. Unemployed
			3. Not known
			4. Not known
			5. Not known
			6. Not known
			7. Not known
Leonardo	Counsellor	Ex-youth worker (step-father)	1. University educated. Working with children with ADHD
			2. College – Music technology
Catherine	Supervisor	Self-employed – capacity not known	No siblings
Richard	Part-time cleaner	Unemployed	1. Schoolchild
			2. Schoolchild
			Half-siblings
			1. Manager
			2. University educated civil servant
Hamish	Not known	Works at Boots	1. Sociology Degree at new university
Mohammed	Not Known – refugee living with extended family. Some enrolled at college		
Leah	Not interviewed		
Jordan	Not interviewed		
Gabby	Not interviewed		
Honey	Not interviewed		
Natalie	Not interviewed		

Figure 13 – Occupational and educational backgrounds of level 1 students' parents and siblings

In Richard's case these were older, half brothers and sisters. Mohammed was a refugee from Somalia and had no siblings in the UK but said that some of the extended family he had here were, 'learning English'.

Mohammed had a complicated background and was the subject of more oppressions than other members of the group. He had arrived in the UK quite recently and still had some difficulty speaking English, which was his second language. In addition to this, he had epilepsy, a heavily stigmatised medical condition, which he said caused him 'understanding problems'. Despite these difficulties, he was the only student in this group who aspired to a professional career (see figure 14), perhaps reflecting different expectations or social status in his homeland. He said that he was 'good at maths' and that he hoped to be an accountant. At the end of the year his highest level achievement was an Open College Network (OCN) numeracy certificate but, since this was at level 1, he clearly faced a very extended transition in order to achieve his aspiration.

Imagined futures

All except one of the career aspirations expressed by the students showed heavily gendered patterns. Only Natalie described a future which, whilst possibly falling into the realms of fantasy, was not gendered in terms of either occupation or lifestyle. She wanted to own a rum bar in Jamaica, and made no allusion to domesticity in the data she contributed. The remaining five female students all made allusions to domesticity. Catherine, Jordan and Gabby all included children and a home as part of their imagined futures and Leah hoped to work as a children's club leader. Although Honey did not describe children as part of her imagined future, she did expect to live 'in a big house, two cats, two dogs' implying some notion of domesticity.

Some students contributed information about themselves which contained an element of confusion in terms of the nature of the aspirations expressed. Honey and Jordan identified lifestyle aspirations rather than occupational aspirations and there was a lifestyle element to some of the occupational aspirations expressed by other students. In most cases this was of a celebrity nature but even where this was not the case, it related to achieving a particular level of material affluence, as in Honey's ambition to 'own a big house'. Other students anticipated even greater levels of affluence. Natalie, for example, stated that:

> I am going to emigrate to Jamaica, have my own Jamaican rum bar, own my own yacht ... I don't know anyone else who's doing it. (Natalie, level 1)

Student	Occupational Aspiration	Do you know anyone already doing this?
Natalie	Own a rum bar in Jamaica	No
Max	Plumber/painter and decorator (apprenticeship)	No
Leah	Children's club leader	No
Jordan	Have children, buy a car, buy a house	Step-aunt bought her house
Gabby	Model with family	No
Honey	Big house	No
Leonardo	To own my own business	No
Catherine	Fashion Designer (Maybe I'll have babies and work in a clothes shop)	No
Richard	Computer technician	No
Hamish	DJ on radio	No
Mohammed	Accountant	No

Figure 14: Occupational aspirations and potential role models for level 1 students

Natalie's family originated from Jamaica and she had spent several holidays there which seemed to have influenced her plans for the future. Where students expressed celebrity lifestyle aspirations, these were readily accepted by other members of the group and appeared to be regarded as possible or even probable realities. This is well illustrated in the following exchange which took place between Leonardo and Catherine:

Leonardo	I want to be a multimillionaire, in fact I don't want to be, I'm going to be a multimillionaire...
	I'm going to be owning my own gym, my own boxing gym as well, my own CD stores, [I'll have] a big supermarket full of CDs
Catherine	Like HMV?
Leonardo	Yes, like HMV
Catherine	Or Virgin
Leonardo	Yes, one of them

Max's lifestyle aspirations related to 'living in [a] mansion' and again were readily accepted by the other students, despite being inconsistent with his expressed occupational ambition of gaining an apprenticeship. Hamish wanted to be a 'DJ on the radio' although he did have a secondary ambition to be a baker 'Morrison's, Asda's, Tesco – somewhere like that'. Gabby hoped to be a model, and could see no dissonance between this and her other aspiration which was to have a family. Jordan was more pragmatic, but still aspired to a particular level of affluence when she identified her aspirations as to 'have children, buy a car and buy a house'. However, Catherine provided a note of rather wistful pragmatism when she talked about becoming a fashion designer, but went on to say that she was more likely to 'have babies and work in a clothes shop'.

None of the young people had a role model who was already working in the occupational area they hoped to move into and, although three did have siblings who had participated in Higher Education, only Mohammed, who ironically was singularly lacking in such a role model, aspired to that level of education. Similarly to the young people at St. Dunstan's College, they were all vague about how they would achieve their occupational or educational aspirations. Catherine expressed the greatest clarity when she reported that it would take 'about five years' to make her transition through Further Education in order to access a fashion design course in Higher Education. Despite this, she was unaware of the credentials she might need or the possible routes she could take to achieve her ambition. Mohammed and Leonardo were even more vague. Talking about his possible educational progression, Mohammed suggested that:

> actually, I think it will be about probably two years after that it will.. [then] I'll go to university, to see how it's going to be there. (Mohammed, level 1)

Leonardo thought that 'doing my [level 2] business course' would provide him with the all skills and knowledge he needed to develop the business empire he dreamed of.

The young peoples' confidence in their ability to achieve their aspirations was undimmed by this lack of awareness, but was not shared by the staff who taught them. Will envisaged a far less rosy future and questioned the whole social and economic value of level 1 courses:

> I am very sceptical about the social and economic value, and I question what we are actually doing. We should not just be baby-sitting, but in fact the programmes we offer do not tackle the underlying problems. We are not equipping

them for the things we should be – preparing them for employment for example ... I think they move into low paid jobs, benefit claimancy, crime and this is because we are not meeting their needs. Will (Lecturer, level 1 programmes)

Will's concerns about level 1 programmes were shared by Jaskaren. Both lecturers worked across a range of vocational programmes from level 1 to level 3. In contrast, those staff who worked exclusively on the new level 1 programme were overwhelmingly positive about the opportunities they considered it offered and focussed on this in their responses rather than addressing what might be perceived as more political questions. For example, Janet (Head of Department) emphasised the opportunity for students to undertake research projects as part of a tutorial programme and described how, 'because these students come from culturally impoverished backgrounds' enrichment activities were provided in the form of external speakers. Janet regarded the programme as a progression route to level 2 although only a small number of students actually progressed in this way.

Jaskaren said that 50 per cent withdrew during the first year and, of those who did complete, two left for 'unknown destinations'. Pat and Gabby outlined another alternative for level 1 students. This was a 'link group for those who don't achieve level 1 during their first year. Where this happens, perhaps for social or confidence reasons, students will have the opportunity to stay on for a further year'.

The fact that this possibility was regarded as an 'opportunity' implied that young people made informed choices to extend their transition at level 1 by a further year. Whilst this may be the case, interview comments made by the students and discussed below seem to suggest that they had little real choice in enrolling on the level 1 programme. This raises the question whether an additional year at level 1 could be defined as 'choice' or 'opportunity', particularly considering the lack of occupational or educational credibility associated with the qualifications achieved by students during their time on the programme.

Choosing a good qualification

None of the students on the level 1 course had originally applied for that programme. Most applied for level 2 programmes but did not meet the entry criteria and were directed to level 1. Those who progressed from special needs provision were directed to the programme. Richard, a student who had previously spent a year on an Entry level provision, reported that '...the head of the Entry course, Elaine, told me about this course and how you could *really* get your maths and English...'. Leonardo, who was undertaking the Art and Design option at level 1, had originally hoped to do a level 2 engineering programme. He had not made an informed choice about his enrolment on the level 1 programme, and explained that:

> [I came on to level 1] 'cos I couldn't get onto the course that I wanted to get onto ... it was engineering, refrigeration and reconditioning. [I came on to level 1] because I didn't know what else to do. (Leonardo, level 1)

Leonardo was not alone in being on a very different programme to the one he had hoped to pursue. Max thought he had enrolled to retake his GCSEs, and only after the course had begun did he realise that he was on the level 1 programme which was, he said ' just where they put me on'.

Despite being on a programme which was not of their choice , all members of the group demonstrated a degree of 'buy in' to lifelong learning. This was illustrated in their recognition of the instrumental value of accumulating credentials of progressively higher value. Their reasons for intending to complete the course were related exclusively to the credential value rather than the course content. Asked what they wanted to achieve from the course the students' responses created a sense that they regarded the programme not as an opportunity to learn, but as a form of time served before they could move on to the programme of their choice.

Max wanted to gain 'qualifications' from the level 1 course, a response which was confirmed by Leonardo. Rob, Richard and Mohammed all intended to use the credential as a basis for progression. Catherine hoped to 'go onto another one [course]' and Max to 'try and get an apprenticeship'. Despite the fact that he was taking the Level 1 catering option, he wanted an apprenticeship in either painting and decorating or plumbing. All the students expected to remain at the same college for future programmes, perhaps demonstrating some recognition of the lack of credibility that the level 1 programme had outside the institution. This lack of credibility was reflected in Leonardo's comment that 'I will use [the level 1 qualification] any way I can use it, I will use it, but I'm not sure where I can use it'.

These views were expressed by students who enrolled during the first year of the level 1 course. During that time the programme had a very high withdrawal rate, a fact highlighted by Jaskaren, one of the lecturers:

> 50 per cent of the intake have fallen by the wayside [this year] due to misbehaviour or non attendance. The level 1 Group [College Management Group] is to look into why they don't attend. (Jaskaren, lecturer, level 1 programmes)

Such high withdrawal rates might possibly be related to the lack of real choice and control during the transition to level 1; alternatively they might be related to the high degree of ambivalence about the programme which was expressed by the students. All the students agreed that the level 1 programme was 'better than school', and the support they received from the lecturers was a key factor in this. However, in terms of the course content and the credential it would generate, students expressed generally negative views and were explicit in placing a low value on the programme. Leonardo and Catherine also said that these views were shared by their parents. Leonardo was frustrated with the bureaucracy involved in enrolling on the programme. Leonardo had wanted to enrol on a level 2 programme which he regarded as a much better option than the level 1 programme, and which was very different in content:

> This is what happened right. I went for the test [to get on to the level 2 programme] and everything and they said they'd get back to me. [After several] days came I rang up to see if I were on the course or not and they said they'd lost my details, so I went in for my test again, came back and I were... you have to ... they still didn't get back to me so I kept having to phone up and eventually they sent me a letter saying I didn't get on the course. So they need to talk to you more. (Leonardo, level 1)

Leonardo's comments suggest that he did not feel valued by the college. His frustration at the lack of communication from the college, combined with his failure to gain admission to the refrigeration programme, was compounded by his mother's belief that he was incorrectly placed on a level 1 programme:

> Well, my mum thinks it's a waste of time to be honest, a waste of time. I didn't get really bad GCSEs but she thinks that I shouldn't be on this course because I am going backwards instead of forwards.

Leonardo said that he had gained Ds and one C at GCSE, and that his mother considered that he should be doing 'something harder'. Catherine's comments suggested that her mother not only took a negative view of the programme but also regarded it as a form of punishment or negative reinforcement: 'My mum says it's my own fault I'm on this course – I shouldn't have messed around at school'.

Experiences such as Leonardo's and Catherine's may also be reflective of the generally low level of value placed on level 1 students by the education system and wider society. Janet alluded to this in comments about the difficulties in marketing the programme, although her comments also implied an informed choice on the part of young people who had not achieved at school:

> Marketing the programme presents particular issues, as the programme is essentially a provision for those who have failed and head teachers/schools like to talk about success. This is a particular issue given the overall results in [this city] at GCSE. Students applying for GCSE re-sits need a minimum of 3xD grades, so this provision appeals to those with lower grades. (Janet, Head of Department, Foundation Studies)

This comment suggests that Leonardo at least, with his one C and several D grades, could have been offered a different course.

All the young people who participated in this study achieved a range of Open College Network (OCN) credentials at the end of the academic year in which the fieldwork took place. Most were achieved at level 1, but Rob and Mohammed achieved the lower level Entry 2 and Entry 3 respectively in literacy. Of the six students who were interviewed, Catherine, Leonardo and Richard all progressed to GNVQ Intermediate or BTEC first Diploma (level 2) provision in a subject of their choice. Mohammed progressed to the pre-GCSE provision whilst Max and Rob both left college, moving to unknown destinations.

Hanging in

The students in this group all expressed some buy-in to credentialism, mainly as disappointment that they were doing level 1 rather than the subject-specific level 2 programme most had applied for and in their intention to progress to level 2 the following year. This was well illustrated in Leonardo's comment that he enrolled on level 1 because 'I didn't know what else to do'. Although Pat (programme co-ordinator) and Gabby (lecturer) stated that 'the majority have part time work', only two of the six interviewed were in employment. None reported having any domestic responsibilities, although the gender split may have been significant here. Only one female (Catherine) agreed to be interviewed and her experience may not have been typical of other young women in the group. It was apparent, however, that all the young people in this group had troubled educational biographies which are discussed below.

Catherine had been excluded for disruptive behaviour and believed that 'the teachers had got it in for me'. Max left school half way through year 9 for reasons that he was not prepared to discuss. Neither achieved any GCSEs. Leonardo had attended school, but had not gained the required GCSE grades to access his preferred programme (engineering, refrigeration and reconditioning). Hamish and Richard both had special educational needs and had been educated in the special schools system. Both had done pre-level 1programmes at college before enrolling on this programme. Mohammed was a refugee, with an unsettled past and disrupted education. English was his second language.

These backgrounds were typical of the group as a whole. Gabby and Pat described the average level 1 student as:

> 16, white; 50:50 gender, inner city who have failed with the education system. They have either been through and failed or not been in at all. The majority are from lone parent families and they experience a variety of economic and social deprivation. Some have had brushes with the law. (Pat, programme co-ordinator, and Gabby, lecturer, level 1)

Jaskaren believed that many of the students' difficulties had their origins in problems at school, and were compounded by a failure on the part of the schools to address those difficulties:

> L1 students mostly had problems at school – schools do not have time to explore or investigate problems and they fell by wayside. Most do not have GCSEs. (Jaskaren, lecturer, level 1)

During classroom observations the students were seen to be conforming to the requirements of the course in that they were making some attempt to complete work that had been set – filling in gapped handouts for example. For much of the time, however, their activity in the classroom related to leisure pursuits, in that much of their learning time was spent chatting and conversation tended to be around leisure activities, something which was common to all students in this ethnically mixed group.

College: a better education

The group on the level 1 programme expressed a high level of ambivalence about their course. At interview they were critical of much of the course content, and this was related to the fact that they were doing something quite different to the programme they had originally applied for. In respect of the content, the group complained that it was 'boring'. However, this criticism related to individual units of study rather than the course as a whole. Mohammed, for example, found the unit on sexual health 'boring' but considered that business studies was 'very interesting' whilst Leonardo had not enjoyed European studies: 'when we were doing about, like, history I was quite interested in that but after that I thought it was boring'. There was a common consensus, however, about the 'learning outcome records'.

Catherine	No the only boring thing is sometimes when you have to fill in all those stupid sheets
Max	Yeah. Learning outcomes sheets and stuff like this
Leonardo	Yeah, Yeah
Max	Then you have to tick, like did you enjoy this lesson? Was it boring? Did you find the work hard or easy? and then write a comment about the lesson

Learning outcome records were completed after every session and normally involved each student completing a pre-formatted A4 sheet which provided evidence of learning activity and was then placed in a portfolio to generate evidence for OCN qualifications. It was time consuming , normally taking the last fifteen minutes of each session and the students' resistance to the activity mirrored that reported in CPVE students a generation earlier (Green, 1991: 190).

Where the young people in the level 1 group expressed positive feelings about attending college, this did not relate to the programme but to their relationships with members of the staff team and the support that was offered by them. This was illustrated by Rob who said that:

> The teachers are really nice ... they help you out and offer you support when you need it, say if you're stuck on a particular maths question or English question and what have you. You stick your hand up and they come and help you. And say you are at school and whatever, you don't get as much support as you do at college, where you get more support and more people are willing to help you and stuff. (Rob, level 1)

These comments were supported by data generated from an activity in which students reviewed and commented on a handout which outlined the emerging themes from the initial data analysis. All agreed with the two statements:

- Many level 1 students did not like going to school
- Almost all level 1 students prefer going to college rather than school. This seems to be because they feel that they are treated with more respect in college

Where the comments were amplified, the preference for college rather than school appeared to be related to the relationship with lecturers, which was perceived to be more equal than that with teachers. Rob, for example, writing in response to both the above statements, said 'True – they prefer college than school because of how they are treated they are treated differently than school' whilst Max believed that the second statement was true 'because people are treated more equally at college' but sadly, in response to the first of these statements responded 'true because if they like it they would have done well and not be on this course'. Leah commented that: 'I agree with what you have said because I agree I hated school'. The students were generally very positive about their relationships with the staff. One or two students did make some negative comments but these related exclusively to the staff response to a littering incident the day before the interviews. This incident led Leonardo and Catherine to complain that 'some teachers are too mardy'.

Similarly to the students, the staff team all made reference to the importance of relationships, which they believed to be a strength of the programme, and placed this in the context of the group's perceived need for nurturing. The difference between relationships in school and in those in college which had been highlighted by the students was also emphasised by Paul:

> I like the relationship between students and tutors. Serious attention has been given to make it different to school and with a fair amount of success. Students do sometimes push it to restore the old balance they are familiar with. The difference between a secondary school teacher and college tutor is that there is more of an equality, as opposed to an authoritarian approach. There is a person centred approach and this facilitates more equality. (Paul, lecturer, level 1)

This 'person centred' approach was apparent in all the fieldwork visits to the college. Individual students spent sustained periods of time talking to different members of staff about issues related to their behaviour or social circumstances. This was also highlighted by Gabby and Pat who considered that: 'their needs are different from the other levels – there is more opportunity for pastoral care. It is a different kind of pastoral care'. The group's perceived need for this type of approach was ascribed by most staff to the social circumstances in which the young people lived, summed up by Janet as 'some have learning difficulties and disabilities, whilst others have experienced difficulties such as a chaotic family background, permanent exclusion, pregnancy, having caring responsibilities or school phobia'.

This 'different kind of pastoral care' extended to the flexible timetable followed by the group, which was much less restricted than in other departments of the college. Gabby and Pat explained how it worked:

> If a lesson is regarded as 'failing' or students are showing lack of motivation we take a break or go to the park to play football. The students do not abuse this- they know that they are expected to work for 20 minutes – football – lunch – more work – they know this is negotiated.

This flexibility significantly limited the time spent on the formal curriculum but also meant that the young people were provided with much more space in which to develop social and leisure aspects of their identity.

Pat and Gabby discussed the students 'needs' in quite general terms. Jaskaren, whilst also subscribing to the general nurturing ethos and expressing the belief that level 1 students were in need of more support, saying that 'almost all students bring baggage and family problems', was more specific about the type of difficulties faced by the students, and also highlighted cultural and ethnic factors which concerned him:

> This was something we found at parents' evening – the kids come with baggage from their family. On parents' evening, we got mostly black and Asian parents – this shows how much support is given.

> The other thing people should look at is general culture in the working class. If my son did better than me I would be proud but I have been to meetings in mining communities where if the son is doing better than dad he doesn't like it. Mining communities used to have a job for life and this engendered the attitude 'I don't need to study' – this attitude still prevails in the third generation. If someone does better the community doesn't want to know. With Asian and black youth it is mostly peer pressure [which leads to low or non-achievement] – they drift into bad habits smoking dope etc. (Jaskaren, lecturer level 1)

Having fun, hanging around

Having sufficient money to pursue leisure and social activities was of fundamental importance to the young people in this group, and this highlighted the importance of social identity in their lives. All the young people who were interviewed were in receipt of EMA or benefits (see figure 15).

Student	Existing Financial support/Employment
Max	Receives EMA Employed to sell 'totally legit' CDs and DVDs at car boot sales
Leonardo	Receives EMA, jobs at McDonalds and on market stall
Catherine	EMA and parental support
Richard	EMA
Hamish	Benefits
Mohammed	Benefits

Figure 15: Sources of financial support for level 1 Woodlands College students

Catherine also received pocket money from her parents for being 'good' which was withheld if she was 'bad'. However, she did not clarify what being 'good' or 'bad' involved. Two of the male students, Max and Leonardo, had part time employment which involved them in the unseen, untaxed, informal economy. Leonardo also worked part time at the local McDonalds. Much of the discussion with Catherine, Leonardo and Max was around material goods – things they wanted and things they had. Catherine was regarded by the others as 'flashy' and 'posh', because she lived in a less disadvantaged area and received pocket money from her parents as a reward for being 'good'. As well as this, her family had three cars. The debate between the three students became quite heated as Catherine rejected Max and Leonardo's accusation that she was 'posh', arguing that 'one is my dad's work car and the whole family clubbed together because she wanted one and brought [sic] my mum a Citroen Saxo'.

This exchange between the students highlighted the way in which material possessions were regarded as forms of status symbol to be aspired to by the group. Max explained that Catherine's home area was 'posh' because 'It's quiet, there's no kids around and all the houses are big, all good cars in the car parks'. 'Good' cars were defined somewhat extravagantly as 'a Bentley' by Max but Leonardo was more pragmatic: 'Not necessarily, a Ford or something like that. Not a Skoda ... a banger like that'.

The main social activity that all members of this group participated in was shopping – all cited this as a spare time activity or hobby, consistent with the value they placed on material possessions. The other activities the group participated in fell into two broad categories – sporting activities such as boxing, (Leonardo), swimming (Richard) and football (Mohammed), and more intimate activities such as spending time with friends playing computer games (Max) or going round to a girlfriend's or boyfriend's home (Rob, Catherine and Leonardo). Most of these leisure activities, particularly shopping and sport, had a significant cost associated with them. This placed demands on the young people to generate sufficient financial capital to participate in what they regarded as essential activities.

The importance of such activities to the group was also evident in the classroom, when their conversation related almost exclusively to money, leisure, possessions and social activity such as nights out and holidays. For example, Natalie talked about her holidays in Jamaica, and Catherine described saving up in her 'decorating my bedroom jar'. No discussion involved learning activities or college work, and attending college appeared to be seen in social terms as, for example, when Rob said that 'I like spending time with my friends at college' and Mohammed that 'my friends and I usually meet at college'.

Summary

Whilst these young people saw themselves as serving time on their level 1 course, they were also using the opportunity to rehearse essential social skills. They were using the friendship networks developed in college, and the time spent there, in the development not of a learning identity – something which was, possibly, on hold until they progressed to a programme of their choice – but in the development of a social identity, which appeared to be a fundamental aspect of their overall identity formation. Perhaps more significantly, this aspect of their development was also regarded as of primary importance by the staff team, whose nurturing approach focussed more on social than educational development.

Hopes for a different kind of future

These three narratives reflect the difficulties and complexities facing young people on lower level vocational programmes as they make the transition from school to work. They also demonstrate the high occupational aspirations held by these young people, and the tensions between those aspirations, their dreams of affluence and celebrity, and their knowledge of career and educational paths. All the young people said they were committed to staying in education and gaining 'good qualifications' but there were tensions here too, this time between learning and the imperative to generate income, and between learning and leisure identities. There were also conflicts between the overt messages about progression and achievement, given by the staff teams as part of the support to develop self esteem, and the more covert recognition by staff that most students would not progress and would face a very different reality to that drawn from government rhetoric about opportunity and lifelong learning. Despite this difficult present reality, all the narratives expressed a hope for a different kind of future.

Part 3
Little stories of hope, dreams, inequality and (lack of) opportunity

It is wealth that perpetuates a constellation of privileges whose central pillar is education (Frei, 2008:267)

The voices of the young people in this study reflect the many layered complexities of their transitions and the dichotomy between the stories they tell and the reality of their present lives and likely futures. Each group is constrained by structures influencing their identities which are beyond their control. In the level 1 group (Woodlands), these might be described as having identities on hold, as they pursue a programme they had not anticipated joining. In the GNVQ IT group (St. Dunstan's) there are constraints arising from racial and cultural stereotypes and aspirations of great affluence. The young women in the HSC group (St. Dunstan's) demonstrate dispositions shaped by female caring stereotypes (Colley *et al,* 2003:471; Clarke, 2002:62-77), aspiring to careers in caring professions but rejecting motherhood and domesticity.

Part 3 discusses what Griffiths (2003:81) has termed the 'little stories' told by the young people. By this, she refers to the fact that such stories are about particular people in specific contexts. The little stories in this final part of the book describe the lives of the young people within the context of oppressive systemic and embodied structures and explore how they use their limited agency to develop identities and negotiate transitions within the constraints imposed by those structures. The book concludes with a consideration of the implications of these stories for policy practice and research in 14-19 education.

8
Classed and gendered inequalities

Introduction

This chapter discusses the classed and gendered inequalities which constrained the lives of the young people in this study. It explores how the young people accepted as natural and normal societal and embodied structures of class and gender which directed them to particular roles and forms of education. For all the young people in this study, gender was a defining characteristic and, like the young women in Bev Skeggs' work a decade earlier, class was 'completely central to their lives' (1997:161).

Culture and Class

The students fell into two main cultural groups. Three quarters (24/32) were white working class with family backgrounds in the ex-mining communities of the Midlands and Yorkshire. A smaller number (7/32), but nevertheless almost a quarter, were the children of immigrants to the United Kingdom. Six of these young people came from Muslim families, a majority of whom originated from Pakistan. All the students involved in the study came from lower socio-economic groups. Although this study was more concerned with class and gender than with race, the numbers of young people from ethnic minority backgrounds indicates that they are disproportionately represented in vocational education. Their social positioning, and the social and cultural practices associated with that, were significant in the development of femininities and masculinities which regarded very traditional, differentiated gender roles as being both natural and normal.

For generations, the white working class mining communities of Yorkshire and the Midlands have been split on heavily gender stereotyped lines. Men went down the pit and did heavy manual work. This was often well paid and did not require any academic preparation – young men left school at 15 or 16 and, until the industrial decline of the 1980s, went into a job for life. Women married young and engaged in domesticity and child rearing, usually within a short distance of their own parental home. Cultural practices like this reproduce the status quo by reinforcing 'belief in the prevailing system of classification' because they are 'grounded in reality' (Bourdieu, 1990:71) forming part of the social structures which constrain us. These traditional values and practices persist in the ex-mining communities today and were highlighted by Jaskaren, a lecturer at Woodlands College. He contrasted white communities with ethnic minority families:

> On parents evening, we got mostly black and Asian parents – this shows how much support is given.

> The other thing people should look at is general culture in the working class. If my son did better than me I would be proud but I have been to meetings in mining communities where if the son is doing better than dad he doesn't like it. Mining communities used to have a job for life and this engendered the attitude 'I don't need to study' – this attitude still prevails in the third generation. If someone does better the community doesn't want to know. (Jaskaren, lecturer, Woodlands College)

This comment also illustrates the differing value placed on education by different social and ethnic groups and it demonstrates the way in which the prevailing paternalistic culture of the former mining communities maintains a status quo in terms of family hierarchy and consequently class status. Discussions about gender often focus on female roles, but father/son relationships which discourage education in this way suggest that it is not only young women who are constrained by local cultural and gendered practices and beliefs which are regarded as natural and normal by the community.

The key characteristics that both the Asian and white working class cultural groups had in common were socio economic status and a strong adherence to traditional gender roles. Class was reflected not only in lifestyle and parental occupation, but very much by the type and nature of the programmes the students were following. Colley *et al* (2003:479) have argued that courses in Further Education are both highly gender stereotyped and populated mainly by students from working class backgrounds. And at lower levels academic options are limited to Basic Skills and GCSE re-takes but vocational options are much more widely available.

Vocational programmes have been widely criticised for socialising students into particular job roles (Bathmaker, 2001) and tend to be regarded as of lower status than academic programmes (Bloomer, 1996:145/148; Edwards, 1997: 1). Gleeson (1996:100) has argued that they are 'typically uncritical' and do not address important issues of inequality and social justice yet, for the young people in this study, a level 1 vocational programme at their nearest college was their only option. They were unable to stay at school (and most would not have wished to do so) as they did not have the pre-requisite credentials to study at a higher level.

Moreover, as a result of policy implemented by a government intent on credentialising the whole workforce, they were denied access to benefits but paid to stay in education. Thus, a decision to go to the local college and take a level 1 vocational course could hardly be considered to be a choice or even the 'pragmatically rational process' described by Hodkinson (1998:103). It was more a case of Hobson's choice, illustrated most poignantly in Max's comment that 'it was just where they put me on'. Employment opportunities for unskilled 16 year olds with low level or no credentials are limited, and vocational training options such as NVQ normally require some evidence of credential even at level 1. In addition, work based training for many occupations (for example plumbing and childcare) is available only at level 2 and above, effectively excluding those young people who do not meet the entry criteria in terms of precursor credentials such as GCSE.

The full extent of these constraints on the choices available to young people with low level or no GCSE passes becomes apparent if consideration is given to the institutions which do offer level 1 programmes, and the variety of options which are available. These constraints influence both the institution attended and the course undertaken. In the case of the Woodlands students, the city is dominated by one large college on multiple sites. The level 1 provision is concentrated at a site on a main arterial route two miles from the city centre, and seven miles from the nearest alternative college provision. Similarly, St. Dunstan's is located at the centre of Townsville, some distance from the nearest alternative provision. Both are readily accessible by public transport.

St. Dunstan's offers a limited range of GNVQ Foundation programmes and, during the year in which this study took place, Woodlands College was in the process of discontinuing GNVQ Foundation with the strategic aim of enrolling all level 1 students on the college's own programme. For all young people, serendipity determines which college is the closest or the easiest to access.

The type and content of programme on offer there is determined by internal policy, and the nature of guidance or allocation to programme is equally open to chance, often determined by factors such as the number of enrolments in a particular year.

Thus, in terms of socio-economic status and lack of credentials, these young people are structurally positioned, perhaps inevitably, to make a transition to low level, low status further education programmes. The range of such programmes is limited and, like all vocational FE programmes, heavily gendered (Colley *et al*, 2003:479). In this way societal structures determine not only that a young person will undertake a low level vocational programme but also the nature of that programme. Hence the HSC group was exclusively female, and the IT group, apart from Emma's brief time on the course, exclusively male. It has also been argued that such programmes prepare young people for specific occupations (Ainley, 1991:103; Bathmaker, 2001) and that this is achieved by instilling behaviours such as attendance and punctuality (Cohen, 1984:105; Chitty, 1991b:104) rather than by education in a wider and more democratic sense, such as the education for studentship described by Bloomer (1996; 1997). The 'learning activities' pursued are 'busy work' – useful for filling time whilst such behaviours are instilled, and able to produce an individual 'socialised to work' (Tarrant, 2001) but of little value in terms of learning and education. For the young people in this study, enrolled on programmes which had an emphasis on social and emotional development rather than learning, it was arguable whether they even acquired development on these lines.

There is no acknowledgement of these realities in government policy and rhetoric which claims to be promoting choice and control over educational options for all young people. This rhetoric fails to recognise either the structural constraints which prevent real choice or the hidden agenda of the need for low pay, low skill workers discussed by Ecclestone (2002:17/19). The economic drivers for education policy are expressed in terms of an idealised post-Fordist rhetoric which fails to acknowledge key societal (and economic) issues, but reinforces existing inequalities in society, since in the context of such an approach:

> Economic needs are placed within a dominant position and the satisfaction of other societal requirements is dependent on the success of the economy. Such definitions of economic need represent the interests of dominant social groupings, namely those of capital, men and white people, and are presented as universal and taken for granted. (Avis, 1996:81)

This subordination of the education system to the economic system where it merely exists as a structure for the reproduction of class (Bourdieu and Passeron, 1977:178/179) suggests that current government economic policy is also performing a class reproduction function by determining through policy and funding mechanisms the type and nature of programmes that are available. The lack of choice and opportunity that directs young people to low status vocational courses suggest that the state is, perhaps unwittingly, complicit in the reproduction of social class in that the education structures and systems serve to fulfil its economic need for low pay, low skill workers, rather than being, as it claims 'an engine of social justice and equality of opportunity' (DfES, 2006:1e).

Gendered roles and domesticity

Socio-economic structures and those of the education system are not alone in denying opportunity to these young people. Adherence to traditional gender roles, or 'gendered habitus' (Reay, 1998:61), in which both young men and young women appeared to view the gender divisions as natural and universal, also formed a major part of the young peoples' dispositions and identities. Thus, the male students in the St. Dunstan's IT group envisaged futures where they would 'look after' a wife or girlfriend and, indeed, a family. The female students, whilst notionally rejecting domesticity as an option for the future, were all engaged in domestic activity at some level and a significant number undertook often onerous caring responsibilities in addition to their college course. This was most evident among the students in the HSC group at St. Dunstan's.

Colley *et al* (2003) have argued that vocational learning is a process of becoming and that 'predispositions related to gender, family background and specific locations within the working class are necessary ... for effective learning'. Further, they suggest that the dispositions of individuals on care programmes are shaped by the female stereotype of caring for others, supporting earlier arguments by Skeggs (1997:56/57) who suggested that a caring self is a 'dialogic production', meaning that it cannot be produced without caring for others.

Such processes were very apparent with the young women in this group. Caring activity itself was clearly heavily gendered among the young people in this study – references to domesticity in the male dominated IT group related exclusively to future marriage and there was no evidence of caring activity on the part of any male student, rather an inferred expectation of being cared for.

However, there was a tension between the HSC students' caring identities (demonstrated in their choice of programme and in their individual caring roles) and their expressed rejection of fulfilling a 'wife and mother' female stereotype. Hodkinson *et al* (1996:117-119) found that, despite entering gender stereotyped occupations, young women made little reference to marriage and domesticity when describing their future plans, and suggested that they were disinterested in marriage and domesticity after observing the impact of this on older sisters. Consistent with this, only three of thirteen students in the HSC group (Brady, Paris and Jennifer) included children in their imagined future and of these only Jennifer thought that the child(ren)'s father might form part of this future. Significantly, these students had no major domestic or caring responsibility within the home, unlike those of their peers who rejected domesticity as a possible future. Another student, Catherine (Level 1, Woodlands) envisaged an eventual domestic future, although in her case it was not what she aspired to but rather an acceptance of a somewhat unpalatable inevitability.

In addition to issues around gender and social class, other characteristics amongst the young people who participated may have increased their potential for social exclusion and marginalisation. These included characteristics such as ethnicity, disability, caring responsibilities and being in care, all of which influenced the context in which they sought to negotiate transitions and develop identities. Of these characteristics, Jaskaren, a lecturer on the level 1 programme at Woodlands, considered ethnicity to be a major influence on educational outcome:

> There are also family issues if ... they don't get any support from white families, whereas black and Asian families try to push them but the culture among Asian Youth is that *not* learning is cool. (Jaskaren, lecturer, Woodlands College)

It is apparent from this comment that significant differences in attitudes to education, and the value placed on it, may be found not only across different cultural and ethnic groups, but also within those groups. Further, where there are differences within groups, such as the Asian group highlighted, that this is as a result of generational conflicts in attitudes to education. There are a number of possible explanations for such conflicts which may have arisen as a result of changes within the community, or as a response to wider youth culture and the increasing value placed on leisure activity amongst all young people.

Ethnicity was not raised by any other participant in the study. It is perhaps significant that Jaskaren, a Sikh of Indian heritage, comes from an ethnic minority background. For Samir (IT, St. Dunstan's), a young man who was confined to a wheelchair and had been educated within the special schools system, disability was a defining characteristic. However, whilst such characteristics may have influenced the identities of some young people who participated in the study, the two key characteristics influencing the identities of all the participants were gender and class. A significant feature of these was that the gender roles adopted by the young people tended to be consistent with the gender stereotypes prevalent in the working class communities in which they lived. Indeed, such is the mediating power of class that it is possible that all other exclusionary characteristics may have been experienced differently had these young people come from more affluent socio economic groups with access to greater levels of cultural and economic capital.

Summary
The intertwined structures of class and gender created invisible and insurmountable barriers for these young people, who were defined in terms of the lack of cultural and social capital associated with their class status, and by cultural expectations of them associated with gender. These structures led to them being directed to classed and gendered forms of vocational education which are deemed suitable for young people from particular social groups and which, whilst offering an illusory promise of opportunity, lead only to low pay, low skill employment, thus maintaining the status quo in a very divided society.

9

Fantasy futures

Introduction

This chapter explores the reality of the futures facing the young people as they negotiate their transitions from school to work and seek to develop identities which are heavily influenced by notions of affluence and celebrity. It discusses occupational futures which are likely to involve renegotiated transitions and to be low pay, low skill occupations rather than the technical and professional roles the young people dreamed of. In this context, their occupational hopes are as fantastic as their dreams of instant wealth and celebrity.

Wealth, celebrity and reality

All the young people in this study, irrespective of gender or ethnicity, demonstrated a fascination with celebrity culture, and a conviction that one day they would experience a sudden transformation which would lead to a celebrity lifestyle. The preoccupation with a celebrity lifestyle formed a significant aspect of the young peoples' leisure activity in terms of their interest in popular culture and the lifestyle of celebrities such as the Beckhams. As well as engaging with media reports on individual celebrities, they also watched a range of popular competition programmes on television in which the winner received significant cash rewards and instant fame, such as *Big Brother* or *X Factor.* This was reflected most strongly in their aspiration to achieve an affluent lifestyle, but also in their choice of celebrity pseudonyms for this study: even those names I was unfamiliar with were eventually established to be those of 'well known' celebrities drawn largely from the fields of sport, film, television or fashion. Ball *et al* (1999:214) have discussed the concept of fantasy futures, a belief in sudden transformation, that one day they will waken up rich and famous (for example by appearing on *Big Brother* or winning the lottery), and this phenomenon has also been identified in a study of NEET (not in education, employment or training) young people in Wales (TES, 2006).

Some young people did, however, acknowledge the likelihood of a more mundane future. For example, Catherine (Level 1, Woodlands) wanted to be a dress designer but recognised that she was more likely to 'have babies and work in a clothes shop' whilst Al (IT, St. Dunstan's) wanted to be an IT consultant in America, but followed this up with the wistful comment that 'I can dream it'.

Whilst the students in this study acknowledged that their futures were likely to be more mundane, they did not appear to see any dissonance between their likely future employment and their lifestyle aspirations. Paris (GNVQ HSC, St. Dunstan's) for example, wanted to be a midwife, but envisaged herself living in 'a mansion' in North Yorkshire. Leonardo (Level 1, Woodlands) expected to become a self-made multi-millionaire. Although his plans for achieving this were somewhat vague, and certainly inconsistent with his occupational ambition to become a refrigeration technician, they were not apparently unrealistic to those who were interviewed with him. This inability to detach an occupational aspiration from a fantasy lifestyle seems to suggest that the young people perceive their occupational ambitions to be as unlikely as winning the lottery.

However, having such dreams, whether of fantasy futures or even fantasy occupations, may be necessary to enable the young person to accept the reality of here and now and to enable them to rationalise pragmatic responses to imperatives such as the need for money. Thinking like this allows the young person to accept a low paid job because there is always the possibility of a return to education or sudden transformation; the mundane reality and drudgery of unskilled work is only temporary in the context of such a rationalisation. This was evident in the fact that none of those students in employment at the time of interview enjoyed their jobs – they regarded them as purely instrumental in providing the money necessary to support themselves, largely in terms of their leisure activities. A perception that low pay, low skill work would only be temporary was also apparent in the interviews with Alice and Rea (HSC ,St. Dunstan's). Both these young women wanted to go to university but both were considering leaving college at the end of the year to 'get some money behind me'. Both anticipated a return to education at some unspecified point in the future.

There is a further dissonance between the students' occupational aspirations and the nature of the programme they are undertaking. The level 1 programme at Woodlands consists of a pic'n'mix of OCN (Open College Network) units at level 1 or below and a limited choice of level 1 NVQ units from four occupational areas. The programme has no national recognition and none of the credentials gained by the young people has any occupational credibility. It is a generic programme and was perceived by the young people as irrelevant to their chosen career.

The GNVQ, which was a vocationally orientated, unitised programme with an outcome-referenced model of design and delivery, did have national recognition, but was lacking in esteem and had little, if any, occupational relevance. At this level, the IT programme included units limited to operating a computer and using different applications, whereas those students who aspired to work in the computer industry imagined futures where they would be engaged in more technical work such as that described by Amir (GNVQ IT, St. Dunstan's) as 'programming. Programmer and stuff like that. Taking computers apart, taking viruses out and stuff like that'. Clearly, acquiring such a level of expertise would require a prolonged skills development and extended transition which would involve moving beyond a familiar habitus (Bourdieu, 1990:52-53) to the unknown, where cultural capital would be 'stretched beyond its limits' (Ball *et al*, 1999:212).

The HSC students are, if anything, in a worse position than the IT students or even those on the level 1 programme. Despite the GNVQ being founded on a notion of occupational competence (Raggat and Williams, 1999:19) the Foundation GNVQ is not recognised as an acceptable credential in the care industry, where government regulation stipulates that the minimum qualification is an NVQ level 2 (Care Standards Act 2000). Employment in the sector is also limited to over eighteens, so for these students, aged 17 at the end of their programme, the only option in their chosen field was to progress to the BTEC First Diploma in Care/Health, or the CACHE Certificate in Childcare.

The minimum entry requirement for both programmes was a Merit at Foundation level. In fact, only five of the thirteen students in the HSC group were expected to achieve this by the end of the programme although two others were predicted to be borderline Pass/Merit. Therefore the credential achieved at Pass not only lacked credibility in terms of employment and wider social perception but also failed to facilitate progression even within the college. This is not unusual – anecdotal evidence suggests that similar criteria are applied at many colleges, largely as a result of inspection and funding pressures to ensure that achievement rates remain high. This raises the question 'what happens to those who do not or cannot progress to level 2'? No reliable data was available for this, as the institutions do not follow up students. However, John (Programme Coordinator, St. Dunstan's) and Will (lecturer, Woodlands) both suggested that such students drift into low pay, low skill work and possibly also, in Will's view, to benefit claimancy and crime.

These would seem to be the likely outcomes for those students who withdraw from their programmes or who do not progress. At Woodlands College, Jaskaren (lecturer, level 1) reported that: '50 per cent of the intake have fallen by the wayside [this year] due to misbehaviour or non attendance' and had gone on to say that a management level investigation was in place to identify likely causes of non-attendance and withdrawal. At St. Dunstan's, Emma, Naz, Wayne, Paris and Rukhsana had difficulties adapting to the GNVQ requirements and, although Wayne did achieve a pass, the others were all unclassified at the end of the programme and moved on to 'unknown' destinations.

In comparison, Brady (HSC GNVQ, St. Dunstan's) was reported to have been an 'excellent' student by her tutor, and had achieved a Merit at the end of her programme but also left college, again to an 'unknown' destination. Despite corresponding to Bathmaker's (2005) description of a 'good' GNVQ student and being in a position to engage with the government rhetoric of lifelong learning, Brady chose to negotiate a different kind of transition. This was, perhaps, in recognition of the fact that her foundation level credential did not 'articulate with work entry' (Slee, 1997:187), at least in the field of Health and Social Care.

The increasing uncertainty about the future, and the decision by some to pursue different paths to those originally envisaged, was also noted by Davies and Tedder (2003) in their case study of a BTEC National Diploma in Health Studies group. The decision to re-evaluate, and to negotiate a different kind of transition, may reflect a pragmatic acceptance that horizons for action (Hodkinson *et al*, 1996) are limited, or what Ball *et al* (2000:135) describe as 'exhausted learner identity'. This is reinforced by a dawning awareness of the likely length of transition to achieve their initial aspiration (seven years each for a degree level occupation such as nursing, teaching or computer science and four for nursery nursing or to achieve a technician level qualification in IT from a level 1 point of entry).

Despite being low level, low status programmes with little occupational relevance, each did potentially provide a stepping stone to an extended transition which, if an appropriate route were followed, could conceivably result in the young person achieving their occupational aspiration; and it is on this basis that so many government policy documents cite 'opportunity'. Similarly to the young people in Bathmaker's (2001) study, however, none of the young people I interviewed demonstrated any understanding or knowledge of the educational route and prerequisite credentials necessary to achieve their aim, nor indeed showed any inclination to investigate this. All indicated an intention to progress to a level 2 programme, even where they were unlikely to meet the entry requirement. This is, perhaps, unsurprising given the lack of other options available to them. Little, it seems, has changed since Clarke and Willis (1984:4) described the move from school to work as a 'transition to nowhere'.

Summary
These young people have dreams of wealth and celebrity which, whilst dissonant with their occupational hopes and ambitions, provide some relief from the drudgery of their day to day life. They have more pragmatic hopes for professional and technical job roles, which would be achievable for most young people but which, in the context of a low level vocational programme, are as unrealistic and fantastic as hopes of winning the lottery and, for some, possibly even less likely than appearing on reality TV.

10

Buying in to learning or working
hard at doing leisure?

Introduction

This chapter explores the dichotomy between the young people's personal rhetoric, which indicated a 'buy in' to their course and the concept of lifelong learning, and other evidence from the study which suggests that leisure, not learning, is of primary importance to young people. It suggests that the rhetoric of lifelong learning is rehearsed by the young people in part because these are the messages they receive from their tutors and institutions, but primarily because they recognise that value is placed on people who learn. Their rhetoric forms part of an attempt to gain societal recognition through engagement with a low level vocational programme.

Rehearsing the rhetoric of lifelong learning

When they were interviewed, all the young people on the GNVQ programmes expressed a clear verbal commitment to 'doing the course' and to the concept of lifelong learning. They all anticipated progressing through an extended transition to a professional or technical role, suggesting that their apparent commitment may have been the instrumental motivation based on a form of credentialism promoted by educators and policymakers described by Ecclestone (2002:20). Commitment to the programme itself was less apparent in the Woodlands level 1 students but, nonetheless, these students also expressed a commitment to the rhetoric of lifelong learning. However, for all those students who participated in the study, this apparent commitment was inconsistent with the other data.

In terms of what the young people said, a picture was created of each individual industriously using their learning programme to build up to the future. Each young person expressed a clear perception that commitment to education, working hard and achieving 'good' credentials was important. This was expressed in a number of ways. For example, Wayne (IT, St. Dunstan's) explained how important good attendance was to success, whilst Rea (HSC, St. Dunstan's) described giving up work to concentrate on the course and Jade (HSC, St. Dunstan's) outlined her plans for progression and future occupation. They all believed they were working hard, and expressed confidence that with continued commitment they could achieve their occupational ambitions.

However, my observations and data from staff interviews indicated that they spent most of their time doing leisure rather than doing work. This contradiction between personal rhetoric and reality was interesting. Most of the young people interviewed were confident and articulate (at least in terms of their ability to discuss dreams and leisure, though less so when they were discussing their education) and did not seem to be expressing the lifelong learning rhetoric because they believed these were the answers I expected, but rather because this was their reality, at least at that moment in time. Possibly then, their apparent 'buy in' to the lifelong learning rhetoric formed, at least in part, a recognition of the societal value placed on credentials and occupations, and reflected an attempt to move beyond the dispositions they brought from past learning programmes (Ecclestone, 2002:144) and to be valued within a hierarchy of lifelong learning.

Bathmaker (2001:90) found that some young people stayed on their programme out of a vague belief in a possible future pay off which 'they expressed as a repeated claim that qualifications will get them jobs'. For those in a position to progress to higher level programmes, as most reported intending to do, there are some grounds for this belief in that even relatively low status programmes and credentials can buy a degree of economic capital. Colley (2006:25), in her study of CACHE Diploma Childcare students, argued that part of the role of Vocational Education and Training (VET) is to allow young women with particular emotional resources to develop and refine them and, ultimately, to exchange them for a form of economic capital, albeit for very low wages, or for more cultural capital but on vocational courses in low status institutions. This argument could be extrapolated to other vocational students on other programmes, and may well be the case for those students who achieve at level 1 and are able to progress to level 2 programmes and eventually into employment.

However, the same cannot be said for those who fail, withdraw or choose not to continue to level 2 and this group forms by far the greatest proportion of level 1 students. Instead, it could be argued that they are making pragmatic decisions such as those described by Hodkinson (1996:125) and exercising agency constructively in the sense that they are recognising the structures and constraints which limit them and are using what little cultural capital they possess as a basis for gaining whatever economic capital they are in a position to secure.

Emma (IT, St. Dunstan's), for example, was working as a cleaner at a local supermarket when she withdrew from the programme. Emma's mother, a cleaner at the same supermarket, had obtained the job for her. Paris failed her GNVQ and, although her destination was unknown to the college, she was working at the time as a packer at a local food processing factory and it seems likely that she continued with this employment which, like Emma's job, had been obtained for her by her mother who also worked there.

It seems that Emma and Paris, like many other young people in similar situations, were simply making the best of the circumstances in which they found themselves. For many young people this will mean using existing capital in the form of family connections to obtain low paid, low skill work which will generate an immediate, if limited, economic return, rather than hoping that a vague and distant future will provide credentials necessary to get the job (and economic return) that they aspire to.

The value of credentials should not be underestimated. Riseborough (1993: 57) has argued that 'Grades are cultural capital passports into higher education and work' and cites Becker's (1968) argument that grades form a currency which supports the economy of campus life. Reay and Wiliam (1999) found that young children viewed the SAT assessment process as a definitive statement about the sort of learner they are. Similarly, lower level students seem to construct success through the achievement of credentials, or 'good' qualifications, which are conflated with the ability to get 'good' jobs.

This was a perception apparently shared by many parents. Two thirds of the students reported parental support as a factor in their decision to go to college. In all but one case, this was associated with parents' aspirations for their offspring to achieve 'good' qualifications and 'good' jobs. Good appeared to be defined in deficit terms, in that it reflected achieving something rather than nothing, where nothing referred to unemployment and parenthood. The possible exception to this was Jennifer (HSC, St. Dunstan's), who said that her mother wanted her to attend college because 'I were slow at school'. In terms of parental support, mothers had a far higher profile than fathers, and this was the same for both male and female students.

However, the type of intervention made was largely abstract, being confined to a general emotional (but rarely financial) support for the young person to go to college, combined with a somewhat vague desire for them to 'do well'. These interventions, well-meaning but lacking in purpose, were similar to those described by Ball *et al* (1999:217) who suggest that, although all social groups report parental support, there are significant social class polarisations in terms of the nature of the interventions made which arise from the parents' own experience of education.

Reay (1998:60) argues that mothers have a more significant role in providing such educational guidance and support and identifies seven aspects of cultural capital which are significant in home-school relationships, including educational background, knowledge and credentials and material resources. None of the mothers (or indeed fathers) of the young people in this study was reliably reported as having educational credentials beyond level 2. Most had limited material resources and, in view of their own educational background, were likely to have limited educational knowledge or resources. Consequently, the mothers of students like those in this study do not have the cultural capital to generate academic profits for their children, and social class reproduction becomes more likely as educational experience and achievement is inherited in the form of cultural capital.

This notion of educational inheritance (Ball *et al,* 1999) is significant because most of these students aspired to a graduate or senior technician level career, but none had any parents with education beyond level 2 and only four participants had any siblings with a university education. Of these four, two students, Hamish (Level 1, Woodlands) and Richard (Level 1, Woodlands) had both been educated in special schools and had formal diagnoses of learning disability, so may not have been typical of the wider group.

Working hard at doing leisure

Part of the commitment to lifelong learning expressed by the young people was reflected in their often-expressed belief that they were 'working hard'. This conviction conflicted both with published research (Bathmaker, 2005:89) and other empirical data arising from the study, yet it was apparent that the students were not inventing this – their insistence that they do work hard was consistent across all groups. Part of this phenomenon may be explained by perception or cultural constructions of work. However, at least part of it seems to be a need to conform, perhaps as a result of the socialisation effect of vocational education alluded to by Cohen (1984:105) and Bathmaker (2005:89).

Across all the groups, the staff teams were concerned with issues of motivation, behaviour, attendance and reliability, and the students were clear that these all held a value in an educational context. Part of the process of hanging in seemed to be a need for the young people to perceive themselves to be conforming to this (and thereby demonstrating their value as members of a learning society), despite the very limited educational value of level 1 programmes and the fact that they behaved 'as if education happens by a process of osmosis' (Macrae *et al*, 1997:505).

The alternative to conforming would have been to acknowledge the likelihood of becoming an outsider to education with all the associated disadvantages. Whilst these young people might not have been able to analyse the effects of social exclusion arising from non-participation in education and subsequent employment in low pay, low skill work, they may well have recognised that such a process would lead to a loss of their imagined future.

It is also worth noting that there were three different ways of interpreting the classroom activity referred to above. The young people believed they were working hard, the staff considered that they lacked concentration and my interpretation was that the students were using the time as an opportunity to negotiate arenas and identities mainly associated with leisure activity. It is apparent that young people experience considerable tension in negotiating between different arenas as they try to reconcile the demands of social lives which are 'pivotal elements of their identities and are equal to, if not more important than, their educational selves' (Ball *et al*, 2000:59) with those of college and learning towards which they have a somewhat ambivalent attitude, and work or domesticity, both regarded as generally unpleasant necessities.

The leisure activity which took place in the classroom was focused on discussions related to social and leisure activities which the young people were planning or had recently participated in. For the HSC students at least, this provided the opportunity to rehearse the communication skills which are fundamental to work in the HSC sector; this was particularly apparent when they utilised those skills to provide mutual emotional support, a feature of group relationships which was absent from both the level 1 and IT groups. Most of this group claimed to 'love college' but the focus of this again was less concerned with the course and more with maintaining the friendships they had formed in their group.

Leisure also provided the imperative to work since the social activities the young people engaged in were all expensive. Communication with friends made the use of a mobile phone essential and the make and model were significant in conferring status. Even hanging around with friends entailed a cost – meeting in town and shopping, or going to a pub or someone's home and drinking alcohol. Alcohol use was consistent across both genders and all cultural and religious groups. Drinking alcohol provided the opportunity to socialise with friends in the evenings, and often at lunch break when many students, in defiance of college regulations, spent time in the nearest pub. Other activities such as dance and sport also entailed a significant financial outlay. However, leisure activity provided a form of light relief, something to look forward to in lives that were perceived by the young people to consist largely of the mundane and boring – college, work and domesticity.

Ball *et al* (2000:68) have discussed the 'choice biographies' emerging amongst more affluent adolescents in which the traditional connected-ness from school to college to work has been broken, but where work, leisure and study are 'balanced' and 'flexible' in order to generate more cultural capital and facilitating the presentation of the transition in a positive light (for example, as a 'good' gap year). The high priority placed by the young people in this study on social lives and leisure indicates that these priorities are common across social class boundaries although less affluent young people such as those in this study do not have the same material and cultural resources to create a positive choice biography as do their middle class peers, and this limits both their ability to participate in education and to consume as members of society.

Despite this, their willingness to invest significant emotional and financial resources into their social lives is indicative not only of the importance they place upon it but also of the fact that these young people too are constructing different biographies, in which their social life forms the most important aspect of their identity, to the extent that learning identities may be abandoned in order to generate the economic capital necessary to pursue social activity. This is consistent with Unwin and Wellington's findings (2001:51) that young people are increasingly seeking out alternatives to full time education and may provide a further explanation for the significant number of students on lower level programmes who fail to achieve or choose not to progress in education.

Whilst many aspects of these social lives were benign, others were less so and concerned behaviour related to reckless sexual activity, the use of illegal drugs and alcohol. Using individual agency in this way leaves young people open to judgements such as 'disaffected', 'disengaged' or 'socially excluded'. Social lives which involve aspects that may be subject to such pejorative discourse are articulated in a particular way. They provide relief from an otherwise mundane life, in which there are almost no opportunities to change the status quo, yet at the same time they provide an opportunity to challenge or resist that status quo by indulging in behaviour which is at odds with a wider and more readily accepted culture in society.

However, placing the greatest emphasis on their leisure rather than their learning identities and exercising their individual agency in this way will not enable them to engage with the system and negotiate a transition to a professional occupation. Instead, they are more likely to develop a form of agency which provides at least an illusion of independence and overtly rejects state sponsored institutionalised education systems. Another form of this is disaffected behaviour in the classroom, stigmatised by government and society but reflecting nonetheless a clear rejection of a system about which many young people have few illusions.

For example, Naz (IT, St. Dunstan's) stated that he preferred college to school because 'it's about being treated with respect and no uniform' but continued to exert individual agency in his rejection of the conformist GNVQ culture. He attended sporadically, spoke provocatively, used class time to pursue discussions about leisure activities and rarely submitted any work. In doing this he reflected an adolescent sub culture which uses dress, language and behaviour 'consciously at odds' with the official culture of the institution and which works in tandem with the schools' distinction between 'good' and 'bad' students as it reproduces the social relations of the wider world (Webb *et al*, 2002:123/124).

Summary

This chapter has considered the data arising from this study and suggests that as the young people involved attempt to develop identities and negotiate their transitions from school to work, a number of things are happening. They are developing identities in which learning, leisure, work and domesticity are intertwined, but where leisure is of the most fundamental importance. Despite the high priority the young people place on leisure, they recognise the importance of learning at an instrumental level – in the sense that it can provide credentials which in turn can lead to improved job opportunities. There is also a recognition of the societal value placed on learning, and what appears to be a need on the part of the young people to be viewed as 'buying in' to learning, something which, of itself, confers a degree of societal value. Despite this apparent 'buy in' most of the young people reject a system which can only offer them an extended transition on low value courses. Instead, many choose to utilise what limited capital they have in return for low skill, low pay work which can finance their leisure and social activities. These are '...not just sub-cultural practices, they are pivotal elements of their identities and are equal to, if not more important than, their educational selves' (Ball *et al*, 2000:59).

11

Nurturing and the needy:
a therapeutic ethos

Introduction

This short chapter discusses the discourse of fragility and the nurturing or person centred approach used with the young people who were all perceived to have an extensive range of social, emotional and behavioural difficulties which warranted additional support. This support took place in the context of both the formal and the hidden curriculum. Staff worked to support the students with aspects of personal development which were often synonymous with the characteristics demanded for low pay/low skill work: attendance, motivation and reliability. Another key focus for the staff was enhancing self esteem, part of which involved rehearsing aspirations and expectations with the young people which suggested that their fantasy futures were in fact realistic and possible.

Staff who are nurturing, students who are needy

Whilst many of the behaviours of the young people in this study might have been described as disaffected, both in the classroom and in their social activity, and some of them (such as Keira, Pete, Samir and Mohammed) had significant difficulties in life which might require professional support, the perception amongst the staff teaching these young people was that they were *all* needy students who required a high level of nurturing and support. There was evidence of nurturing at some level in all the groups participating in this study, reflected in the language used to and about the students, the acceptance of certain behaviours and the willingness to offer support for students' problems; this suggested that the staff had bought in to a discourse of fragility. There was a higher level of nurturing in the HSC group which could be ascribed to staff backgrounds in that all members of that team had originally trained in the caring professions, predominantly in nursing.

The ethos could be regarded as part of the 'therapy culture' described by Furedi (2004) in which marginalised and disaffected young people are regarded as vulnerable and in need of support. Strategies to address these perceived problems may include support as part of an educational programme, whether integrated formally in the sense of engagement mentoring described by Colley (2003), or informally as part of the staff team or institution ethos. The discourse of fragility used by the tutors on this programme emphasised such an ethos. Sue (HSC lecturer, St. Dunstan's) described individual students as 'maturing as a person' and considered that the students' social backgrounds were significant in their perceived disaffection and low achievement:

> A student that probably hasn't achieved at school, various reasons, some have the ability but maybe they haven't liked the teacher or the subject, a lot of other pulls on them from studying, personal issues, demands at home, sometimes not having a stable home, two adults and two children, that sort of background.

She also referred to the importance of the social development which took place alongside the formal curriculum and which she regarded as having equal importance to assessed work:

> I think certainly understanding one another in the class, when they're all trying to shout at once and they get argumentative, and they're falling out, I think that's very much a part of the learning that apart from a topic that they'll be tested on or they do an assignment on, with myself or the senior personal tutor maybe, looking at how to get on with others.

Both Sue and John identified 75 per cent of their group as having 'special needs', with John also suggesting that these students would 'need further support and if they don't get it in college they will need it in the community'. At Woodlands College, both Pat and Gabby had emphasised the students' 'low self esteem' and Paul had placed great importance on the 'person centred approach' taken by the team. Similarly to the HSC team at St. Dunstan's, they all subscribed to a discourse of fragility and a nurturing ethos was fundamental to the way the team operated. In contrast to the HSC team however, the Level 1 team came from very diverse backgrounds, none of which involved working in the caring professions.

Clearly, many of the young people who participated in the research had significant personal difficulties which they could not deal with alone. Keira had caring responsibilities with little respite, Samir had significant levels of disability, Mohammed had health problems and the difficulties associated with being a refugee. Pete may or may not have had difficulties associated with the loss of his mother. For other students, though, life was, superficially at least, much more stable. Al, Amir, Catherine and Naomi all came from apparently secure family backgrounds and had the potential to progress to higher levels of Further Education as well as some limited cultural capital which might support a transition to work.

A nurturing ethos tends to attribute similar levels of need and vulnerability to all even where this may not be the case, and may be perceived as part of a growing therapeutic culture within education and society at large. Within this culture, issues such as perceived failures or disaffection are excused on the basis of a broad range of medicalised terms such as low self esteem, trauma or depression (Slee, 1997; Furedi, 2004). This therapeutic culture has been criticised by Ecclestone (2004) who argues that, despite the rhetoric of emancipation and empowerment associated with such approaches, they have in fact resulted in a diminishing of the self and erosion of individual autonomy.

Apart from concerns around demoralisation and the diminished self, there are other, more pragmatic issues concerned with this type of ethos and discourse which were apparent with the young people in this study. In college, well-meaning attempts were made by the teaching staff to promote achievement and raise self esteem. These may be counter-productive. Because teachers work on increasing self esteem, it is possible that the young people are concentrating more on rehearsing unreal aspirations than on generating more cultural capital. Unreal aspirations in terms of both career possibilities and lifestyle, combined with a touching conviction that one day, they will experience a sudden transformation which will change the *status quo*, combine to enable these young people to retain some degree of hope in a very uncertain future.

Conversely, however, the rehearsal of these unreal aspirations also contributes to the structures which confine them to particular places in society – where unrealistic aspirations are rehearsed and cultural capital is not generated, potential for agency is limited and, far from the young people experiencing the sudden transformation they hope for, they remain confined to allotted places in society and maintain the *status quo*.

Summary

This chapter has considered the little stories of the young people in the context of the emerging debate on therapeutic education. Staff teaching vocational students are committed and well-meaning but 'buy in' to a discourse of fragility which attributes similar levels of need to every young person. Whilst some students have significant levels of individual need, others come from more stable and supportive homes and the levels of support they are offered may be unnecessary. As part of their attempts to meet students' perceived needs, staff focus on developing self esteem, where students are encouraged to rehearse aspirations which, in the context of their programme and other structural constraints, are often just impossible dreams which provide some hope in a very uncertain future.

12

Conclusions

Introduction

The dichotomy between impossible dreams and the grim reality of a predestined life is the overriding theme emerging from this study. Two other, more subtle but equally powerful themes have emerged. The first of these is the low value placed upon lower level vocational credentials in terms of their lack of vocational or academic credibility and, by extrapolation, the low value placed upon those young people who undertake these programmes or achieve the credentials. The second is the discourse and practices associated with therapeutic education which serve to place significant limitations on young peoples' potential for agency and contribute to the structures which confine them in their pre-destined place in society.

Impossible dreams

In terms of impossible dreams every young person who participated in this study wanted to do well and to get good qualifications and all had high aspirations suggesting some 'buy in' to credentialist rhetoric. Despite this, they engaged in a range of behaviours which conflicted with their expressed hopes and intentions. These included dropping out, engaging in leisure activity in class, generally behaving as though they could learn by osmosis and frequently failing to conform to their course requirements.

However, their aspirations are no less valid because of this, rather this tension illustrates all too clearly the way in which the wider education system and more specifically the field of vocational education serve to prepare young people for particular roles in life according to their socio economic status meaning that, at lower levels, they are 'warehoused' and offered a 'therapeutic pedagogy' (Ecclestone and Hayes, 2008:76) which can only lead to low pay,

137

low skill work rather than the technical and professional roles they dream of. This is in stark comparison to those young people who undertake academic courses of study which offer very different life and occupational opportunities. Despite government policy which is full of rhetoric about equality (DfES, 2003b:18; DfES, 2006:3) and the low status of vocational education (DfES, 2005:17) there has been a marked failure to address these issues of social justice.

At lower levels only a prescriptive and instrumental curriculum exists, which is far removed from the conditions needed to engage with an education for citizenship and studentship such as those described by Esland (1996) and Bloomer (1996; 1997). Such programmes have little occupational relevance and offer only an extended transition with a vague promise of something better. This opportunity is increasingly rejected by young people who regard it as a transition to nowhere and choose – inasmuch as they have a choice – instead to utilise their limited agency in a transition to the field of low pay/low skill work completing a self fulfilling prophecy which destined them to be prepared for this type of occupation and positioned at a particularly low level within the socio-economic hierarchy. This position is unlikely to change as a consequence of the introduction of the specialised diploma, which carries with it the inequality ridden legacy of ancestor credentials such as GNVQ, and which has been developed in an unchanging political, educational and social context.

Structure and agency, dreams and reality

If considered in isolation and at a superficial level, the activity in the field of vocational education looks positive. During the course of this study the students' articulated a commitment to lifelong learning and achieving good qualifications. Without exception, all the groups were taught by highly skilled and committed teachers who wished only to improve the opportunities and life chances available to their students. Yet this is not sufficient. The field of level 1/2 vocational education cannot be viewed in isolation because it exists within other, larger fields, all of which – wider vocational education, 14-19 education, the whole field of education, the fields of class and power which surround that – constrain the agency of the young people undertaking lower level vocational education. Within these broader contexts, what these students are doing and achieving carries little currency and holds no value beyond the immediate field. By extrapolation, these young people are themselves perceived to be of little value (Castells, 2000:165). Othered as having 'failed' at school, as vocational students, low level students and as disaffected and disadvantaged, they are regarded as the 'embodiment of deficit' (Colley, 2003:158).

Thus within this field, and with limited existing cultural capital at their disposal, the possibility of moving beyond the field depends on the young people developing the agency (and capital) to enable them to negotiate the structural forces which appear to be irresistible barriers to movement beyond the immediate field/habitus. Developing these abilities would require them to receive a better education – to be exposed to a different kind of pedagogy which, in contrast to the busy work which prepares them only for particular kinds of employment, would offer two things: the 'intellectual discipline' or subject knowledge advocated by Ecclestone and Hayes (2008:142/143), and a political education which will enable them to

> understand why they desire the destinies they pursue; to ask critical questions about what those destinies both offer and demand; and to ask why their education contributes so often to the reproduction of social inequality. (Colley, 2006:27)

These are not new concepts: Avis (1996) highlighted the need for a more political education for citizenship and Bloomer (1996:161), addressing issues of empowerment, autonomy and democracy in education, made similar arguments suggesting that existing provision 'disenfranchises young people as citizens and as workers through the 'dependency culture' which it engenders by its institutional discourse'. For young people on more contemporary programmes such as those who participated in this study, the need for significant change remains and must be addressed if we are to have any hope of creating a more just education system which provides real opportunities for all young people. This imperative raises practical and philosophical questions about the nature of education, and whether, instead of considering what a good vocational education might be like, or indeed whether a good vocational education is a possibility, the debate should centre more strongly around the ideal values and content of a good education.

Despite the constraints imposed by class, gender and lack of credentials, the young people in this study were fundamentally no different from any other group. Their hopes and aspirations in terms of career are no different to those of other young people although their attitude to learning is perhaps somewhat more ambivalent. Their prospects of achieving those aspirations are, however, significantly handicapped in terms of the fact that they have no notion of how to achieve them. Likewise, their leisure and social identities, fundamental to their biography construction, are strikingly similar to those of their more affluent middle class peers described by Ball *et al* (2000:69). What sets this group apart is the extent to which they are oppressed by structural forces beyond their control, and the way in which this so often results in a particular use of individual agency – not in the continued pursuit of cultural capital on a low level vocational course and through progression to higher level courses, with their promise of improved lifestyle and greater economic capital, but in a pragmatic decision to generate immediate, albeit severely limited, economic capital.

Such a situation is an indictment of the education system which has prepared them so well for a role as a low paid, low skilled worker that no other option is possible. The bitter irony of using agency to obtain employment is that it results in a further stigmatisation and othering of these young people as dropping out and failing to engage with education, placing more constraints on their already limited agency as they are problematised still further. Thus, the reality for this group of young people is that their high occupational aspirations are impossible dreams, in the same way that their lifestyle aspirations of fame and affluence are impossible dreams.

For some, the failure to achieve their occupational aspirations will mean accepting a 'second best' option, for example in employment as a carer in a residential home rather than training as a nurse, For others, it will mean more casual and possibly less secure work, often in the informal economy. In either event, the gap between their aspirations and likely outcomes in the labour market are clearly highlighted, just as they were for an earlier generation of young people in Bates' research (1993b:77-78). And so is the far more mundane nature of the lifestyle that will accrue from the low pay/low skill alternative they eventually pursue.

Doing leisure

The mundane lifestyle which some young people, in moments of clarity, recognised as inevitable was alleviated for all of them by engagement in social lives and activities. It is apparent that social and leisure activity is the aspect of these young peoples' lives to which they attach the greatest importance. This has also been found in previous research (see Bates, 1993:47; Ball *et al*, 2000:66) although the nature of the social life itself continues to change and evolve.

Much of the leisure activity the young people participate in is related to contemporary celebrity and materialist culture, such as that promoted by the media as WAGs (footballers' wives and girlfriends) culture and involves activities such as shopping and participation in sport. Such activity also provides confirmation to them (if any were needed) of the possibility of sudden transformation, for example through the medium of reality TV shows such as *Britain's Got Talent*. Their hope in sudden transformation bears a marked similarity to the hopes of the masses of earlier generations who relied on the prospect of eternal life as a reward for the endurance of poverty and hardship in this life. In this more secular society, the lottery and reality TV appear to have replaced eternal life as the hope for the future.

From a social perspective, leisure activity is key to being part of a group. This was most apparent in the case of Samir, who insisted that 'I always do what they do' when talking about participating in leisure activities with his cousins and, in the case of Keira, also a case study in exclusion, who just hoped that in the future, apart from caring for her mother she would still 'be [friends] with these three'. However, apart from group membership and the engagement with celebrity culture, it is also apparent that participation in leisure activities impacts on young people's lives in other, less obvious ways. It is a factor in the construction of gendered identities and the tendency to drift into low pay/low skill employment. It was evident that much of the leisure activity the young people participated in was gender stereotyped. For example, many of the sporting activities (eg football, dance and snooker) were clearly gendered and a number of female students, though no male students, spent part of their leisure time rehearsing domesticity in the care of young children.

The financial costs of participation in leisure are significant, and many of the students in this study worked in order to generate the money to support a social life. Whilst this provided them with a tenuous hold on the world of work, it was a hold on a low pay/low skill (and not always strictly legal) world of work which was unlikely to generate much in the way of economic return or career opportunities. Despite this, it did provide a temptation to leave college and work to generate immediate economic capital rather than deferring gratification in the vague hope of a better future at the end of an extended educational transition.

All the activities the young people participated in involved socialising – talking and communicating with their friends. Great importance was attached to this and it was an activity which extended to all areas of their lives including the classroom. It was apparent that, amongst these young people, leisure identities were most significant in the development of overall identity construction, whilst learning identities formed only a small part of this, and then had to fit in with their social identity. In the case of the HSC students, such activity could be argued to have some relevance to the subject taught, as they rehearsed communication skills which are fundamental to workers in the HSC industry. This was recognised to an extent by some HSC tutors but, for other tutors across all groups, such behaviour was generally regarded in deficit terms as a failure to engage or to concentrate. Thus socialising or engagement in leisure can also come to form part of the deficit model of vocational students which, together with its role in engagement with low pay/ low skill work and the reinforcement of gender roles, suggests that the leisure activities which provide such pleasure are actually contributing to the formation of additional structural barriers to using their agency to move beyond a familiar habitus.

The education system must acknowledge the importance of leisure in the developing identities of all young people, something which reflects the increasing importance of leisure in society as a whole, but which currently is only found in the extra-curricular clubs, holidays and other activities for the students at high achieving schools following an academic curriculum. In another example of the inequalities facing young people pursuing vocational courses in low status institutions, the enrichment activities on offer are funded by outcomes, placing inevitable constraints on the type of activity which can be made available. Ball *et al* (2000:146-148) have highlighted the failure of government policy to acknowledge the importance of leisure within its 'utilitarian version' of the contemporary young person, something which is reflected in the existing vocational curriculum. Further, the utilitarian concept of the young person, which views individuals purely as economic functionaries, fails either to value the individual or to recognise wider social and cultural needs and changes, contrary to the notions of social justice the government claims to espouse.

Nurturing and the needy

The evidence from this study suggests that in the field of lower level vocational education, teaching staff work from a position in which students are considered to have low self esteem as a result of the economic, social and educational difficulties they are perceived to have experienced. This humanistic stand-point, which also problematises lower level vocational students, demands that teachers work to give 'unconditional positive regard' (Rogers, 1983;1961) and use humanistic counselling skills in their communications with students. It generates a therapeutic mindset which is concerned with raising self esteem as a way of resolving social problems and which has been widely criticised (Emler, 2001; Furedi, 2004; Ecclestone, 2004; Ecclestone and Hayes, 2008). Such an approach was apparent amongst the staff teaching across all three groups in this study. They were often more concerned with addressing social problems, raising self esteem and developing social skills, than with the content of the subject(s) being taught.

However, one aspect of this is that staff/student relationships are superficially positive and this appears to be a factor in college being perceived as 'better than school' as in Naz's (IT, St. Dunstan's) statement that 'it's about being treated with respect'. On its own, however, this is a simplistic explanation and positive relationships are probably the products not only of a nurturing approach considered by learners to confer respect but also to 'changing dispositions to learning' as motivation is influenced by transition (Ecclestone, 2002:128/129).

A nurturing approach and the incremental individual achievement of low level academic skills will not, of themselves, offer the tools for young people to achieve their aspirations but rather, excessive nurturing will result in a belief on the part of the young person that they can achieve anything without questioning how they will accomplish it, and in a form of dependence on those teaching staff offering support. The result of this is that challenging aspirations – which would include any aspiration involving an extended transition – are not achieved, and the focus of attention becomes the individual, rather than the structural forces which are constraining them. This is consistent with Ecclestone's (2004:118) argument that presenting failure as emotionally damaging results in a belief that the disaffected and marginalised cannot cope without support, in a shift of attention from inequalities in the structure of the education system to a focus on people's feelings about it and to lower aspirations where these are challenging or risky.

Therapeutic discourse defining young people as needy, disaffected or marginalised uses a deficit model which allows both state and society to problematise them as in need of help, an approach which fails to acknowledge the structural inequalities in the education system which resulted in them being so labelled in the first place. Those who are labelled early within a deficit model such as disadvantaged, disengaged and disaffected are more likely to receive support from a superficially sympathetic state, and hence increase the sense of reliance and the social acceptability of dependency to the extent of, in some cases, pathologising certain behaviours within a medical discourse (Slee, 1997:181). Within such a model, young people are encouraged to see themselves as victims, and thus their agency, as the personal autonomy and motivation to change their situation is reduced still further.

Once young people are stereotyped into a passive, submissive role of this nature, it becomes easier to accept it than to challenge or change it and resist 'the oppression of apparent kindness' (Corbett, 1990:3). The acceptance of a low status victim role rejects the agency of individual accountability and autonomy and the young person fulfils the role of a victim requiring help; consequently there is no basis for respect for that individual (Ecclestone, 2004:128). It may also be argued that this contributes to the lower value placed on these young people in comparison to others who are perceived to be independent, high achieving and lacking in vulnerability.

It has been suggested that such superficial empathy and concern for low status groups can rapidly become moralistic and judgemental, as the disaffected and disadvantaged are portrayed and perceived as 'other' (Ecclestone, 2002:26; Colley, 2003:118) and although some aspects of disaffection may be seen as legitimate resistance on the part of the young person (Colley, 2003: 77/101; Corbett, 1990:2), they are more usually associated with a deficit model discourse associated with more negative societal perceptions of disaffected behaviour. Therefore, society labels these young people as 'disengaged' or 'disaffected' and this form of othering results in the problematisation of the individual and not the system, allowing any blame for non-achievement or perceived failure to be attributed to the individual who has failed to engage. This diverts attention from any critical consideration of the system since it obscures the existence of systemic and structural failures which confine people to an allotted place in life, constrain individual agency and replicate social class and other social inequities.

Classed and gendered inequalities

Ball *et al* (2000:145) have argued that new labour market conditions and structures have served to create new class hierarchies, inequalities and exclusions. These exclusions are still reinforced by the English education system which has historically reproduced class structures and ensures that young people reach the age of 16 with credentials and education appropriate to class specific occupations. Those with lower level credentials and from lower socio-economic groups are largely directed to Vocational Education and Training (VET), which has been argued by Bates (1993:72) in the 1990s and by Colley *et al* (2003:491) a decade later to be significant in the replication of classed and gendered inequalities. Such inequalities are highlighted in the data arising from this study in which all the participants were undertaking class specific courses and had parents who had low levels of education and were either economically inactive or employed within class and gender stereotypical occupations.

When discussing the conventional distinctions between 'men's work' and 'women's work' in the manufacturing industries, Ainley (1993:23/24) argued that these were being eroded by the contraction of traditional industry and the expansion of the service sector. Despite these observations, and the length of time since they were made, rigid gender divisions were apparent in this group of young people. Those divisions were evident not only in terms of their lifestyles and attitudes but also in the context of the course they had chosen and the occupation they aspired to, all of which were constrained by class and gender, thus reflecting Hodkinson *et al*'s argument (1996:148) that individual schematic views of the type of jobs an individual may or may not do are developed within a class-based and gendered habitus, meaning that choices are constrained by these factors. Such constraints, in addition to those imposed by other exclusionary factors such as disability, ethnicity and the hierarchy of the education system, which places VET students firmly at the bottom, serve to limit agency and restrict opportunities.

Although Bourdieu and Wacquant refuted the argument that habitus is a fate, arguing instead that it is an 'open system of dispositions' which is 'durable but not eternal' (Bourdieu and Wacquant, 1992:133), it could be argued that, for most young people who fail in the English education system and end up on a level 1/2 course post-16, at the bottom of the educational hierarchy and so also at the bottom of the 'economy of student worth' (Ball *et al*, 1998), habitus is indeed a fate. Constrained by classed and gendered dispositions and expectations and placed at the bottom of the hierarchy of the education system, these young people have no opportunities to move anywhere other than onto the next low status vocational course or into low skill, low pay employment. In these circumstances, it is unsurprising that they focused their lives around leisure rather than learning.

Despite the massive inequalities evident amongst all the students who participated in this study, individual young people shine out as examples of injustice and inequity and raise uncomfortable questions about the nature of our society. In a rich and developed country in the 21st century, should a 16 year old young woman really be acting as the sole full time carer for a terminally ill parent? Would this expectation have arisen had she been male instead of female? Should a young man of 16 be resigned to being 'married off' and 'looked after' on the basis of his physical disability, rather than looking forward to exercising his agency through education and employment? What notions of equality allow young people of only 16 to enter post compulsory education with 19th century notions of gender roles they consider to be universal and natural?

This was not a longitudinal study, and some of the young people interviewed may hang in through a much extended transition to achieve their original aspiration, but this seems improbable given such circumstances and expectations. What is more likely is that, similarly to the young people described by Colley *et al* (2003), Ball *et al* (2000) and Bates (1993a;b) they will revise their plans and negotiate different transitions, with different – and probably lower level – occupational outcomes from those they had originally planned. These are likely to reflect and replicate both their concept of gender roles and the socio-economic status of their parents, thus preserving the existing, inequitable status quo.

Credentials – buying in to learning?

It was apparent that most young people were on their programme as a result of serendipity rather than choice; those young people who had progressed from special needs provision had been directed to particular programmes, whilst those who had applied to college post-GCSE were largely on the programme by default, having failed to meet the entry criteria for their preferred course. For the GNVQ students, this meant that they were studying at a level below the one that they had hoped for, although most were undertaking programmes in a subject area they had chosen. Where this was not the case, young people had been sold alternatives in a different subject area. Emma (St. Dunstan's), who had wanted to do GNVQ Leisure and Tourism Intermediate, for example, enrolled instead on a GNVQ Foundation IT. The level 1 students at Woodlands College had even less choice, being directed to a generic programme with some vocational input in a choice of four areas. In only a very few cases did these reflect the subject in which the young person had originally hoped to study.

Despite this, all the young people in this study had what amounted to a desperate desire to achieve a good qualification, and for most, this was also a parental aspiration. Both students and their parents conflated good qualifications with good jobs – perhaps rehearsing the rhetoric of government policy (eg DfES, 2003b:18). Despite its lack of currency beyond the institution, the GNVQ did have limited credibility in that it was, and to an extent still is, a nationally recognised brand. The GNVQ students and their families appeared to equate 'good' with 'recognisable'. The level 1 offered at Woodlands College does not have a similar level of recognition, and was broadly disliked by the students, possibly because it lacked recognition or branding. Where credentials are perceived by young people to be so critical to future life chances, they need a level of national recognition which in itself confers value on the credential and, by extension, on the individual who is undertaking it.

All the young people interviewed perceived A*-C grades as 'good' GCSEs – once again repeating government rhetoric. Only a small number had achieved one or two 'C' grades, none had achieved As or Bs and most had a profile of F-U. As a result they inferred that they had 'failed' at school (Working Group on 14-19 reform, 2003:11) and that they were inferior to those who had succeeded in meeting the 5 x A*-C benchmark.

For any credential to be considered to have even minimal occupational relevance it must be at minimum level 2 (DfES, 2003b; DfES, 2006:4), leaving as the only worthwhile option for these young people a progression from level 1 to level 2. Yet even this progression up the low status vocational ladder is denied to many young people by the addition of further artificial barriers, such as a requirement to achieve Merit at level 1 in order to meet the entry requirements for level 2. The vocational nature of level 1 programmes also means that eventual access to higher education courses will be more difficult, should any student succeed in completing a much extended transition. Whilst they may achieve a raft of vocational credentials at different levels, they are unlikely to gain the English and Maths GCSEs which are entry requirements for many university programmes. The ongoing TLRP study *Degrees of Success* has shown that students with combinations of vocational and academic qualifications are more likely to access Higher Education successfully than those holding only vocational qualifications (Hoelscher and Hayward, 2008:20). In addition, VET students are more likely to attend less selective Higher Education institutions. In this way, vocational education, particularly at lower levels, is being used to accommodate young people to current economic conditions and to meet the demand for a 'new periphery' (Ainley, 1993:40) of temporary workers, a group forming the bottom, marginalised 30 per cent of our society who are either idle or working for 'poverty wages' (Hutton, 1995:14).

Opportunity – the great deception

Successive governments, whilst acknowledging the impact of social exclusion and perceived educational failure in the form of the lack of a minimum level of credential, have nonetheless placed young people categorised in this way into a deficit model (Major, 1990:23; Colley, 2003:27-28), whilst simultaneously rehearsing a rhetoric of opportunity which suggests that any young person can be or do anything providing they engage with the opportunities on offer. The potential opportunities alluded to in this rhetoric are, however, heavily circumscribed by economic policy and market forces. Crucially, they are all also vocational in content, ostensibly to address skills shortages within 'the powerhouse of a high skills economy' (DfES, 2006:1). Further, the paper makes no attempt to hide where choice and control really lie:

> As we give learners more control over their own learning experience we need to ensure they are making choices only between valuable options which meet employers' skills requirements (DfES, 2006:41 my emphasis)

To put it another way, the 'opportunities' are a limited range of low level vocational courses. A range of papers identifies level 2 credentials as being the minimum for employability (eg DfES, 2003b, 2006; DIUS/DCFS, 2008). The 2003 paper created an invisible group of learners – those undertaking level 1 programmes who were only referred to in terms of not having achieved level 2. The 2006 paper, however, proposes the introduction of a Framework for Achievement (FfA) (2006:43) incorporating a new foundation learning tier, to be introduced from 2013. This continues to assume, however, that young people will progress through the proposed 'coherent progression routes' to 'level 2 and beyond' (DfES, 2006, 2007), and so fails to acknowledge the impact of exclusionary characteristics and the constraints on individual agency of many of the young people working at or below this level.

The young people in this study expressed a commitment to learning which was grounded in a desire to achieve good qualifications and a belief that they were indeed working towards a good qualification, reflecting a 'buy in' to the post Fordist rhetoric that credentials will facilitate engagement with the opportunities available in the new economy, and fulfil the promises of a brighter, better future for all, based on continual up-skilling and engagement with lifelong learning.

They were undertaking courses that they had chosen and continued to make very significant, albeit limited, choices throughout the programme, associated with whether to remain on the programme or leave, whether to work or not, whether to continue on to level 2 or to seek employment. It was apparent, however, that the young people were in fact making choices that were not their own, but were pragmatic decisions 'influenced by the complexities of the relations of force within a particular field' Hodkinson (1998: 103) and which were 'heavily circumscribed by class' (Bloomer, 1996:148).

Therefore, the notion of choice as utilised within policy documents does not exist for these students, since it assumes independent, rational choice made in response to the opportunities available to young people. In fact, as is illustrated in this study, these young people are opportunity-less, but are sold the rhetoric of a post-Fordist dream. This is not merely rhetoric, it is the basis of a massive immorality, a great deception which is perpetrated on young people. They are prepared for and directed to low level vocational courses which by any definition are of limited value, but are encouraged to believe that they are on a good course which will enable them to achieve good qualifications from which they can achieve anything they want.

In fact, the formal curriculum at this level occupies young people with busy work – activities which were criticised by some of the students themselves as unchallenging and which are of very limited educational or occupational value and focuses more on personal development and enhancing self esteem. The immorality associated with the mirage of choice and good credentials is then compounded by the emphasis on support and pseudo-therapeutic interventions which, as Ecclestone (2004) has argued, make the student feel valued and respected, but paradoxically increase their dependency and reduce their autonomy. In doing this, the individual's agency is further constrained and their place in society's hierarchy confirmed.

Such support is offered in the context of programmes such as GNVQ foundation and its successor qualifications which score at a fundamentally low level in terms of preparation for employment and economic or societal value. Programmes such as these are offered to young people as opportunities but in fact teach the skills necessary for low pay, low skill work such as punctuality and conformity. The reality is that the only opportunity available to a student holding a level 1/2 broad vocational credential is progression to a level 3 broad vocational credential – they hold no credibility beyond the institution (Bathmaker, 2001).

Thus, at a fundamental level we are deceiving and manipulating the young people enrolled on such programmes by offering a mirage of impossible dreams, and by giving the impression that they are readily achievable, rather like large sums of money on television games shows. The reality, of course, is that the systems, structures and practices serve only to keep each individual in their allotted place in society. The ultimate immorality is that when, as is inevitable, young people fail to achieve the impossible dream, blame is attributed by the state to the individual (Ainley and Corney, 1990:94-95) for failing to meet their perceived civic responsibility of engaging with lifelong learning.

13
Implications for policy, practice, research and social justice

Introduction

The study has demonstrated the impact of valuing some members of society more highly than others. It has suggested that those young people undertaking lower level vocational programmes experience a range of characteristics associated with social exclusion and are in danger of becoming further excluded from a system where raising standards equates to achieving credentials, rather than providing an educational system which facilitates each individual to achieve their potential and their aspirations. I have likened this exclusion to a form of invisibility from policy makers, funding bodies, employers and wider society.

Working within a social justice framework, this chapter proposes structural and pedagogical changes which would provide a more socially just context for the education of 14-19 learners, particularly those undertaking vocational education programmes at lower levels. The chapter consists of three main sections – implications for policy, practice and research. Each point is suggested as an active way of 'doing justice' as part of the journey towards 'making justice' (Walker, in Griffiths, 2003:125).

Implications for Policy

The longer term policy implications of this study suggest that there should be a fundamental reversal of the government philosophy, followed since the Great Debate, that economic policy should drive education policy. This would involve a rejection of the notion that 'the satisfaction of economic requirements can fulfil other needs' (Avis, 1996:81) and would instead focus on the 'notions of social justice, citizenship and difference [which] are central to the construction of alternatives' (Avis, 1996:80/81). Such alternatives would be predicated on the concept of a good education for all, rather than main-taining artificial divisions between vocational and academic education, when, in reality, the two are synonymous – you cannot take the practical out of science, or be a mechanic without a basic understanding of maths and physics. This should be done in the context of an overall reduction in policy initiatives in the 14-19 sector, providing more time for formal evaluation of policy outcomes. In addition policy makers should:

Consider the use of language in policy documents. This consideration should be given in recognition of the power of discourse and the way in which the use of particular descriptors – disaffected, disengaged, disruptive – result in the othering of particular groups and the attribution of particular charac-teristics to individuals. A helpful move in thinking about the discourse used would be that proposed by Colley (2003:169) in thinking of social exclusion as a process which society inflicts on the disadvantaged, rather than as a set of characteristics to be attributed to them. This more socially just way of con-sidering issues of social exclusion would help to move policy from a position which attributes blame to young people for perceived shortcomings, to one in which the unequal societal structures and processes which create exclu-sion are recognised and addressed.

Consideration of the use of language must not, however, be limited to a re-thinking of the discourse around social exclusion, but should extend to the use of policy rhetoric around concepts such as choice and opportunity. Currently, these terms are used in policy documents which are directed at specific groups of young people – those who already experience characteris-tics associated with social exclusion – and, as this study has shown, much government rhetoric such as that around opportunity is illusory and decep-tive, offering only vague promises which are unlikely to be fulfilled.

In reality, the choice and opportunity available to different groups (eg those pursuing an academic education and those pursuing a vocational education 14-19) are widely divergent and lead to unequal life opportunities which are not compatible with social justice. It would be more helpful to avoid, or at least to clearly define, the use of such problematic terms, and to detach them from the achievement of specific credentials.

In this way, consideration can be given to what choice and opportunity might really mean to a young person struggling against oppressive and unequal societal structures, and to ways in which they might be helped to realise their potential for agency. Policy makers should also recognise that if a young person withdraws from a programme, or chooses not to progress through multiple layers of vocational qualifications, it is not due to an inherent failing on their part (or that of their teachers) but to the challenges of complex lives, the demands on them to generate economic capital and the fact that transitions are not straightforward and predictable, but individual, varied and messy and powerfully mediated by class and earlier educational experiences and (non) achievements.

Provide clear and comprehensive careers advice and guidance for all young people. The stories of the young people in this book suggest that any advice and guidance they might have received was ineffective and that many were directed to particular programmes, possibly for institutional convenience, rather than provided with the means to make a more informed choice about future study and career options. More informed Careers Education and Guidance (CEG) would enable young people to have clearer understandings of possible pathways and outcomes, making it more likely that seemingly impossible dreams might, for some at least, become future realities. Implicit in such guidance would be the acknowledgement that some pathways have very different outcomes to others, and that there will always be a need for some workers who are willing to do casual work for low pay. In this way, issues around the illusory nature of concepts such as choice and opportunity might also be addressed.

Undertake a meaningful re-examination of the purpose and content of the vocational curriculum at lower levels. This would include a consideration of the value of a very broad and superficial curriculum as well as considering what would be a good education: this book suggests one which focuses on subject knowledge and political awareness, both of which might be precursors to more effective vocational education. Perceived disengagement need not be a reason to offer a low value alternative curriculum – the young people in this study believed they were more motivated at college, and much of this seemed to be related to improved relationships and changing dispositions to learning associated with the transition from school to a form of adult education, rather than to the content of what they were doing. Exploiting changing dispositions to learning could potentially be more effective in enabling young people to realise their potential for agency than providing a low value vocational curriculum, and the Further Education sector is ideally placed to provide a model for good practice in doing this.

A re-examination of the curriculum at these levels would revisit the recommendations of the Working Party on 14-19 Reform (Tomlinson Committee) (2004) and the Nuffield Review of 14-19 Education (2006) with specific reference to creating a more coherent and equitable curriculum. It would also review and re-consider the implementation of the 2005 White Paper, which, whilst acknowledging that Level 1 is an achievement for many young people, also introduced the concept of a GCSE Diploma, requiring five A*-C grades including English and Maths and thus diminished the value of a level 1 specialised Diploma. Where credentials are awarded, irrespective of level, they should have national branding and recognition, something which was an important feature of the GNVQ for the young people in this study who undertook it.

Make policy initiatives more inclusive and sensitive to the context of lower level students and the challenges facing them. This could be addressed by some of the developments outlined above, but also by the implementation of a revised funding regime which provided equity of funding across programmes and types of institutions, thus placing a clear value on *all* learners, and which allowed funding for enrichment activities to be detached from specific outcomes and credentials. This would provide greater flexibility for institutions to provide a broader range of activities and experiences to enhance the existing curriculum and generate greater cultural capital for these young people.

Take a less centralised approach to the curriculum. If young people are to be offered greater cultural capital and greater potential for agency, then teachers too must have greater potential for agency than is possible within the current context of instrumental, centralised curricula. There are significant tensions between the centralised control of the curriculum and initiatives such as personalisation – irrespective of whether teachers subscribe to this contested concept – a personalised approach for each learner is impractical within the context of current curriculum constraints and the fact that achievement is, in funding terms, related to outcomes from that centrally controlled curriculum.

Implications for practice

The long term implications for practice would involve a repositioning of vocational programmes and the implementation of a more socially aware pedagogical model in which 'individual and social transformation are synonymous' (Ecclestone, 2004:117) and young people are enabled to develop their capacity for individual agency in order that they can make a contribution both to society and to the deconstruction of structures which militate against social justice. Such a system could also provide the basis for education programmes which 'motivate, inspire and empower' (Ecclestone, 2002: 12), recognise achievement, reduce the barriers to progression and move away from existing perceptions of lower level vocational programmes as remedial or lacking in value, even by those who deliver them (Bathmaker, 2002). In the shorter term, despite the constraints of an instrumentalist curriculum, there are still practice based developments which would contribute to addressing some of the issues raised in this book and which might be implemented by teachers, managers and other practitioners in the 14-19 sector.

Think carefully about the kind of language you use to describe your learners. It is easy enough to do this, simply by posing yourself a few questions. Is the language I am using attributing a particular persona to this group or this young person? Am I assuming that they are disaffected, disruptive or vulnerable? Are they really any of those things? What could they do if I thought about them differently? For those readers who are sure that they only ever see their students as individuals, each year I do an activity with trainee teachers which asks them to think of the group they teach most often and to list five words on a post-it which best describe that group. At best, 70 per cent are negative terms such as those listed above. This realisation, which comes when the trainees sort their words into negative and positive lists, is always shocking to them, but illustrates how easily we come, often unconsciously, to see certain groups in a negative light. Thinking about the language we use in this way is something we can all do to make justice and also helps us, as practitioners, to move from a mindset which sees young people in deficit terms to one which is more focussed on their potential for agency.

Acknowledge the importance of leisure, which is fundamental to the developing identities of 14-19 students. This would involve acknowledging the importance of part time work, and could take the form of careful timetabling. Although the 14-16 curriculum must cover five days, a full time post 16 course is currently only sixteen hours per week. Timetabled over three or four days, this could provide a 'space' for young people to undertake part time work. Associated with this, managers should consult with programme teams to determine the types of enrichment provision which would best meet the needs of students, in terms of generating cultural capital rather than measuring outcomes and, where possible, implement their recommendations.

Ensure that young people have access to as much information about education and career options as possible. Tutorial sessions could be used as a vehicle to explore the implications of taking up employment, as opposed to those of remaining in education. If sufficient detail such as potential and actual levels of income or length of potential transition were discussed, young people would be in a position to make more informed choices about whether to remain in education or move to employment. In colleges, information about transitions to particular occupations should be readily available within programme areas. The lecturers working in a particular area are likely to be most knowledgeable about potential occupational routes in that area. This information could take the form of tutorial sessions similar to that described above, or research activities in which learners identify an aspiration and then explore possible routes to that occupation, or simply in the form of wall displays showing different possible trajectories and equating specific job roles with likely income. Any of these activities would, hopefully, preclude other young people from being as ignorant of how to achieve their goals as were those in this study.

Read critically. Engagement with literature and research offers an opportunity to do justice by developing deeper understanding of the social and political issues related to education and the lives of the young people who are living the 14-19 agenda. In a sector which has a focus on instrumentalist outcomes and is heavily constrained by government policy, it is all too easy to implement the latest initiative and not question it in any way. Critical reading and reflection on that reading provides a space in which we can come to question some of the policies and practices which form the fabric of 14-19 education. All these policies and practices have potential for good and ill. Only by questioning them from an informed perspective can we recognise – and begin to *make* justice by confronting – the systems and processes which militate against young people by contributing to unequal educational structures.

Reflect critically on your own practice. Not just in terms of whether or not the planned outcomes for a particular lesson were met, or how effective you are at managing behaviour – although these things are important – but in the context of wider practice. Question assumptions and taken-for-granteds, for example, that all lower level students are vulnerable and in need of support or that low achievement should be equated with limited potential. Some young people will be vulnerable, but others may not be helped by generating a culture of dependency. Some will be operating at the limits of their ability in achieving level 1 or 2. Others will have the potential to achieve at the highest academic levels or the potential for great success in a particular occupational role. Question the discourse you use and the expectations you have of each student. Remember that treating any group as homogenous, rather than seeing individuals, is contrary to notions of inclusion and social justice.

Implications for research

Research takes considerable time to move from the planning to the publication stage. The implementation of the current 14-19 agenda is relatively recent so it is unsurprising that there is limited research in this area. However, the Nuffield Review of 14-19 Education (http://www.nuffield14-19review.org. uk/) draws together a range of research, including earlier studies in the fields of VET and PCET, as well as publishing issues papers which offer valuable insights to all those concerned with this phase of education. The most recent of the projects informing the Review are those supported by the Teaching and Learning Research Programme (TLRP available at: http://www.tlrp.org/), most notably *Transforming Learning Cultures in Further Education* (TLC), which is now concluded, but also including a range of other VET and PCET projects.

Despite these major initiatives, 14-19 and the wider PCET area remain underresearched in comparison to other phases and areas of education. Where research is published, much of the focus has traditionally been on young people operating at level 3 as part of the parity of esteem debate. Limited and often small scale research has been carried out which focuses on young people at lower levels. A further issue is the need to explore and identify more effective means of dissemination. Although studies such as those outlined above are widely published, publication tends to be for a specialist audience and wider dissemination – for example amongst the professionals working with young people – rarely occurs.

This study indicated that both young men and young women were heavily constrained by gendered identities. Despite vocational education being widely acknowledged to be gender specific, limited work exists on the impact of gendered identities. Apart from Willis's 1977 work, most work in this area focuses on changing dispositions in working class young women training to work in care (Bates, 1993a, 1993b; Skeggs, 1997). Later work on gendered identities in vocational education also has a similar focus (see Colley *et al*, 2003 and Colley, 2006). Although there is work on males in vocational education, this tends to focus on underachievement, particularly of black males. Little attention has been given in recent years to developing masculinities and femininities as a part of overall identity formation within a vocational education context.

There is also a paucity of research exploring the choices and opportunities for young people who participate in the alternative curriculum and their trajectories through vocational education (a single TLC paper addressed 14+ education – see Davies and Biesta, 2004). There is some evidence, however, that young people are directed into particular options at 14+ and that this decision is made for them based on their perceived level of ability (Bloor, 2008). This is supported emerging findings from a study by Colley *et al* (2008). Earlier work by Fuller and Unwin (2003) also tends to support this contention – they found that employers believed that schools do not promote the Modern Apprenticeship (MA), do not encourage young people to apply to non-traditional sectors, and do not do enough to inform young people about the sectors in which it is available.

Research related to how the trajectories into and across vocational education are managed by young people and professionals is also lacking, although Colley *et al* (2008) do suggest that there may be a 'bias of self interest' in IAG provided by schools and other providers leading to 'ill-advised choices' by young people. This suggests that there is a need to explore these issues in depth and over time. Further work might also consider the impact of gendered and classed stereotypes in educational and employment choices made at 14+ with particular reference to the impact of social class on gendered dispositions.

Further work is needed to explore the transition experiences and developing identities of learners at lower levels. Outcomes for young people entering the lowest levels of vocational education are virtually absent from existing research, despite the high numbers of young people involved, and the low retention on these programmes. A longitudinal study would provide data to confirm whether shorter term studies are correct in their suggestions that many of the young people on low level programmes end up in low pay/low skill employment. Other work should evaluate the impact and outcomes of alternative curricula, such as that developed at Woodlands College, to inform the debate around what might constitute a good education. Finally, future work expanding on the findings of this and similar studies could explore the longer term impact of the therapeutic culture in education. This should focus most particularly on young people on lower level programmes who are likely to be more exposed to a therapeutic culture than their more educationally successful peers.

Conclusion

This study has illuminated the complex lives of three groups of 14-19 vocational students. One of the aims of the study was to explore the learning identities of these students. It has found that these are at best very fragile, and that other aspects of identity formation are infinitely more important in the transitions of these young people. Leisure activity and social identities are of the most fundamental importance, with aspects such as gender identities, particularly amongst young women acting as domestic apprentices, also being of great importance. Within the great scheme of things, in these lives, learning identities are of minor importance.

It has been demonstrated that all these young people experience a multitude of oppressions in the face of an elitist and class based society. These various oppressions have shown to include social class, gender, race, disability and education. Education has been discussed in terms of three key issues: firstly, the credentialist nature of the system as a whole, secondly, and more specifically in terms of vocational education and its socialisation of young people to specific forms of employment through the use of busy work – activities which fill time but are of scant educational value. Finally, the nurturing and therapeutic culture in the classroom has been explored.

Characteristics such as class, gender and vocational education serve to bind each young person more firmly into their allotted place in society – one where they are unqualified, low paid, low status and unvalued. This study has highlighted the irony that whilst these young people have the same hopes, dreams and aspirations as their more educationally successful middle class peers they are more constrained by fundamental structural forces and lack the agency and cultural capital to realise their aspirations.

There are particular tensions between the participants' high aspirations and their limited knowledge of the education and credentials necessary to achieve those aspirations, as well as between their verbal commitment to education and lifelong learning rhetoric and other behaviours which indicate a more ambivalent and instrumental view of education. These tensions are key factors in that most of these young people drift into low skill/low paid employment, failing to fulfil their aspirations but maintaining a *status quo* in terms of social class structures. With no real choices and limited agency they are more likely to respond to the limited attraction of any employment which provides an immediate economic return than to invest in a low level, low status vocational programme which offers at best a vague and insubstantial promise of something better at the end of a very extended transition.

Unreal hopes of something better than mundane low pay/low skill employment and the lifestyle that that can support, rely on sudden, almost miraculous transformations which could place the young person in a position in which they had no financial concerns and would facilitate their engagement with leisure activity, whilst simultaneously causing them to be held in a higher regard by the rest of society – valued more, rather than valued less. Yet, within this context, current government policy (DfES, 2006:1) still claims to be 'an engine of social justice and equality of opportunity'. Unless, it would appear, you happen to be a 14-19 vocational education student in England, structurally positioned, partly inevitably, to make choices that are not your own and to do low level activities and be busy (rather than engaged in learning) as a preparation for low pay, low skill employment.

This study suggests that there is a need to acknowledge the structures which contribute to social reproduction in order to consider ways in which a more equitable form of education could effectively promote the realisation of agency and autonomy in all young people. This would involve a debate which could only take place alongside societal changes in which society recognised the need to work towards a state of social justice. Fundamental to this would need to be a societal recognition that individuals must be valued on something more meaningful than their GCSE results and potential economic value, and a governmental recognition that honesty and morality should underpin all aspects of policy. This would involve a significant policy shift from the position we have been in since Callaghan's Ruskin speech, where economic policy drives education policy, to one in which education policy stands alone, predicated on educational and not economic values. Such changes would avoid the great deception called opportunity being perpetrated on future generations of young people.

Finally, the outcomes of this study highlight the need for further research in this area to generate a greater understanding of the complexities of the lives and identities of young people, in order to facilitate a more constructive policy context and to aid the development of a more equal and inclusive 14-19 education system which might enable at least some of these young people to realise their dreams and aspirations.

References

Abbot, Walter M. SJ and Gallagher, Msgr. Joseph (eds) (1966) *The Documents of Vatican II*, London: Geoffrey Chapman

Abbott, I. (1997) Why do we have to do key skills? student views about general national vocational qualifications in *Journal of Vocational Education and Training,* 49(4) p617-630(14)

Ainley, P. (1991) Education for Work. In C. Chitty, (ed) *Changing the Future,* London: The Tufnell Press

Ainley, P. (1993) *Class and Skill Changing Divisions of Knowledge and Labour,* London: Cassell

Ainley, P. and Bailey, B. (1997) *The Business of Learning: Staff and Student Experiences of Further Education in the 1990s,* London: Cassell

Ainley, Pat and Corney, Mark (1990) *Training for the future: the rise and fall of the Manpower Services Commission,* London: Cassell

Allen, Martin (2007) Learning for Labour: specialist diplomas and 14-19 education *FORUM: for promoting 3-19 comprehensive education [online]* volume 49 no.3, pp. 299-304 available at: http://dx.doi.org/10.2304/forum.2007.49.3.299 accessed 17 September 2008

Aristotle (1988) *The Politics* (ed Stephen Everson). Cambridge: Cambridge University Press

Aristotle (1911/1998) *Nichomachean Ethics.* New York: Dover Thrift Editions

Avis, J. (1996) The Myth of the Post-Fordist Society in Avis, J. *et al, Knowledge and Nationhood Education, Politics and Work.* London: Cassell

Avis, James (2007) *Education, Policy and Social Justice: learning and skills.* London: Continuum

Ball, SJ; Maguire, M and Macrae, S. (1998) Race, Space and the Further Education Market Place' in *Race, Ethnicity and Education* 1(2) p171-189

Ball, S.; Macrae, S. and Maguire, M. (1999) Young Lives, diverse choices and imagined futures in an education and training market in *International Journal of Inclusive Education* 3 (3) p195-224

Ball, S.J. Maguire, M. and Macrae, S. (2000) *Choice, Pathways and Transitions Post-16 New Youth, New Economies in the Global City.* London: Routledge/Falmer

Bates, I. (1984) From Vocational Guidance to Life Skills: Historical Perspectives on Careers Education in I. Bates *et al, Schooling for the Dole.* Basingstoke: Macmillan Publishers Ltd.

Bates, I. (1993a) A job which is 'right for me'? Social class, gender and individualisation. In: I. Bates and G. Riseborough (eds) *Youth and Inequality.* Buckingham: Open University Press

Bates, I. (1993b) When I have my own studio ... the making and shaping of 'designer' careers'. In: I. Bates and G. Riseborough (eds) *Youth and Inequality.* Buckingham: Open University Press

Bathmaker, A-M (2001) 'It's a Perfect Education': Lifelong Learning and the Experience of Foundation-level GNVQ Students in *Journal of Vocational Education and Training* 53 (1) p81-100

Bathmaker, A-M (2002) Wanting to be Somebody: Post-16 Students' and Teachers' Constructions of Full-Time GNVQ in a College of Further Education. PhD Thesis, University of Warwick

Bathmaker, A-M. (2005) Hanging in or shaping a Future: defining a role for vocationally related learning in a 'knowledge' society' in *Journal of Education Policy* 20 (1) p81-100

British Broadcasting Corporation (2006) *School leaving age may be raised [online]* available at: http://news.bbc.co.uk/1/hi/education/6135516.stm accessed 12.01.2009

Becker, H. (1968) *Making the Grade.* Chichester: John Wiley

Bloomer, M. (1996) Education for Studentship in Avis, J. *et al, Knowledge and Nationhood Education, Politics and Work.* London: Cassell

Bloomer, M. (1997) *Curriculum Making in Post-16 Education The Social Conditions of Studentship.* London: Routledge

Bloomer, M. and Hodkinson, P. (1997) *Moving into FE: the Voice of the Learner.* London: Further Education Development Agency

Bloomer, M. and Hodkinson, P. (2000) Learning Careers: continuity and change in young people's dispositions to learning in: *British Educational Research Journal* 26 (5) p583-597

Bloor, P. (2008) An investigation into the views of school aged young people engaged in work related education and their perceptions of the opportunities this presents them. Unpublished MA Dissertation, Nottingham Trent University

Board of Education (1938) *Report of the Consultative Committee on Secondary Education with Special Reference to Grammar Schools and Technical High Schools* (Spens Report). London: HMSO.

Board of Education, (1943) *Curriculum and Examinations in Secondary Schools* (Norwood Report). London: HMSO.

Bourdieu, P. (1980c) *Questions of Sociology.* Paris: Les Editions de Minuit

Bourdieu, P. (1990) *The Logic of Practice.* Cambridge: Polity Press

Bourdieu, P. (1993a) *Sociology in Question.* London: Sage

Bourdieu, P. (1996/92) *The Rules of Art.* Cambridge: Polity Press

Bourdieu, P. (2000) *Pascalian Meditations.* Cambridge: Polity Press

Bourdieu, P. and Passeron, J-C. (1977) *Reproduction in Education, Society and Culture.* London: Sage

Bourdieu, P. and Wacquant, L. (1992) *An Invitation to Reflexive Sociology.* Chicago: University of Chicago Press

Brockington, D. White, R. and Pring, R. (1985) *The 14-18 Curriculum: Integrating CPVE, YTS, TVEI? Discussion Document.* Bristol: Bristol Youth Education Service Ltd.

Brooks R. (1998) *Staying or Leaving? A literature review of factors affecting the take-up of post-16 options.* Slough: NFER

Callaghan, J. (1976) *Towards a National Debate* speech given at Ruskin College, Oxford October 18 1976 [online] available at http://education.guardian.co.uk/thegreatdebate/ accessed 24.08.2008

Castells, M. (2000) *The Information Age: Economy, Society and Culture Volume 3: End of the Millennium* 2nd Edition. Oxford: Blackwell Publishers Ltd.

Child, Lydia Maria (1833) *An Appeal on Behalf of that Class of Americans Called Africans.* Allen and Ticknor (digitised version available online at http://books.google.co.uk/books accessed 20/02/2007)

Chitty, C. (1991b) Towards New Definitions of Vocationalism. In Chitty, C (ed) *Post-16 Education Studies in Access and Achievement.* London: Kogan Page

Clarke, J. and Willis, P. (1984) Introduction in I. Bates *et al, Schooling for the Dole the New Vocationalism.* London: Macmillan Publishers Ltd.

Clarke, Julia (2002) Deconstructing Domestication: Women's experience and the Goals of Critical Pedagogy. In R. Harrison, F. Reeve, A. Hanson, and J. Clarke (eds) *Supporting Lifelong Learning. Volume 1: Perspectives on Learning.* London: Routledge/Falmer and Open University

Coffield, F. (1999) Breaking the Consensus: Lifelong Learning as Social Control in *British Educational Research Journal* 25 (4) p479-499

Cohen, P. (1984) Against the New Vocationalism. In I. Bates *et al, Schooling for the Dole the New Vocationalism.* London: Macmillan Publishers Ltd.

Colley H. (2003) *Mentoring for Social Inclusion: a critical approach to nurturing mentor relationships.* London: RoutledgeFalmer

Colley, H. (2006) Learning to Labour with Feeling: class, gender and emotion in childcare education and training in *Contemporary Issues in Early Childhood* 7 (1) p15-29

Colley, H.; James, D.; Tedder, M. and Diment, K. (2003) Learning as Becoming in Vocational Education and Training: Class, Gender and the role of Vocational Habitus in *Journal of Vocational Education and Training* 55 (4) p471-497

Colley, H.; Mazzei, L. and Lewin, C. (2008) The Impact of 14-19 Reforms on the Career Guidance Profession: a disrupted community of practice. Paper presented to the Annual Conference of the British Educational Research Association, Heriot-Watt University (5 September 2008)

Corbett, J (1999) Special Needs, Inclusion and Exclusion in A. Hayton (ed) *Tackling Disaffection and Social Exclusion Education Perspectives and Policies.* London: Kogan Page

Corbett, J. (1990) Introduction in J. Corbett (ed) *Uneasy Transitions: Disaffection in Post-compulsory Education and Training.* Basingstoke: The Falmer Press

Corbett, J. (1997) Young People with Special Educational Needs in S. Tomlinson (ed) *Education 14-19: Critical Perspectives.* London: Athlone Press

Dale, R. (1985 ed) *Education, Training and Employment: Towards a New Vocationalism?* Oxford: Pergamom Press

Davies, J and Tedder, M. (2003) *Becoming Vocational: Insights from Two Different Vocational Courses in a Further Education College.* Transforming Learning Cultures in Further Education Project [online] available at http://www.ex.ac.uk/education/tlc accessed 10th May 2006

Davies, J. and Biesta G. (2004) *Coming to college: the experience of vocational learning of two cohorts of 14-16 year olds in a further education college.* Paper presented to the Annual Conference of the British Educational Research Association, Manchester (September 2004)

Dearing, R. (1996) *Review of Qualifications for 16-19 Year Olds Full Report.* SCAA

Department of Communities and Local Government (2007) *Indices of Deprivation* [online] available at: //www.communities.gov.uk/communities/neighbourhoodrenewal/deprivation/deprivation07/)

Department for Children, Schools and Families (2008) *Promoting achievement, valuing success: a strategy for 14-19 qualifications.* Norwich: The Stationary Office

Department for Education and Skills (2002) *14-19 Extending Opportunities, Raising Standards.* London: The Stationery Office

DFEE (1999) *Learning to Succeed: a new framework for post-16 learning.* London: The Stationery Office

Department for Education and Skills (2003a) *14-19 Opportunity and Excellence.* London: The Stationery Office

Department for Education and Skills (July 2003b) *21st Century Skills: Realising Our Potential Individuals, Employers, Nation.* London: The Stationery Office

Department for Children, Schools and Families (2008) School and college achievement and attainment tables available at: http://www.dcsf.gov.uk/performancetables/ accessed 14 December 2008

Department for Education and Skills (2005) *14-19 Education and Skills.* Annesley: DfES Publications

Department for Education and Skills (2005) *Realising the Potential: a review of the future role of Further Education Colleges (Foster Review).* Annesley: DfES Publications

Department for Education and Skills (2006) *Further Education: Raising Skills, Improving Life Chances.* Norwich: The Stationary Office

Department for Education and Skills (2007) *Raising Expectations: Staying In Education and Training Post-16.* Norwich: TSO

Department of Education and Science (1991) *Education and Training for the 21st Century: The Challenge to Colleges.* London: HMSO

Dewey, J. (1916) *Democracy and Education.* New York: Free Press

Disraeli, Benjamin (1845) *Sybil or the Two Nations.* [online] available at: http://www.ibiblio.org/disraeli/sybil.pdf accessed 15.01.2009

Ecclestone , K. (2007) Resisting images of the 'diminished self': the implications of emotional well-being and emotional engagement in education policy in: *Journal of Education Policy* 22 (4) p455-470

Ecclestone, K. (2004) Learning or Therapy? The Demoralisation of Education in *British Journal of Educational Studies* 52 (2) p112-137

Ecclestone, K. (2002) *Learning Autonomy in Post-16 Education The Politics and Practice of Formative Assessment.* London:Routledge/Falmer

Ecclestone, K. and Hayes, D. (2008) *The Dangerous Rise of Therapeutic Education.* London: Routledge

Edwards, T. (1997) Educating Leaders and Training Followers. In Edwards, T.; Fitz-Gibbon, C.; Hardman, F.; Haywood, R. and Meagher, N. *Separate but Equal? A Levels and GNVQs.* London: Routledge

Emler, N. (2001) *Self Esteem: The costs and causes of low self worth.* York:YPS

Esland, G. (1996) Education, Training and Nation State Capitalism Britain's Failing Strategy. In Avis, J. *et al, Knowledge and Nationhood Education, Politics and Work.* London: Cassell

Fine M.; Weis, L.; Weseen, S. and Wong, L. (2000) For Whom?: Qualitative research, Representations, and Social Responsibilities. In N. Denzin and Y. Lincoln (eds) *Handbook of Qualitative Research* 2nd Edition. London: Sage Publications

Fine, M. (1994) 'Dis-stance and Other Stances: Negotiations of Power Inside Feminist Research' in A. Gitlin (ed) *Power and Method.* London: Routledge

Finn, D. (1984) Leaving school and growing Up. In I. Bates *et al, Schooling for the Dole.* Basingstoke: Macmillan Publishers Ltd.

Finn, D. (1985) The Manpower Services Commission and the Youth Training Scheme: a permanent bridge to work? In R. Dale (ed) *Education, Training and Employment: Towards a New Vocationalism?* Oxford: Pergamom Press

Frei, Matt (2008) *Only in America.* London: 4th Estate

Fuller, Alison and Unwin, Lorna (2003)Creating a 'Modern Apprenticeship': a critique of the UK's multi-sector, social inclusion approach in: *Journal of Education and Work* 16 (1) p5-25

Furedi, F. (2004) *Therapy Culture: Cultivating vulnerability in an uncertain age.* London: Routledge

Galbraith, J.K. (1992) *The Culture of Contentment.* London: Sinclair-Stevenson

Gitlin, A. and Russell, R. (1994) Alternative Methodologies and the Research Context. In A. Gitlin (ed) *Power and Method political activism and educational research.* New York: Routledge/Falmer

Gleeson, D. (1987) (ed) *TVEI and Secondary Education: a critical appraisal.* Milton Keynes: Open University Press

Gleeson, D. (1989) *The Paradox of Training: Making Progress Out of Crisis.* Milton Keynes: Open University Press

Gleeson, D. (1996) Post-compulsory Education in a Post-industrial and Post-modern Age. In Avis, J. *et al, Knowledge and Nationhood Education, Politics and Work.* London: Cassell Education

Great Britain (1903) *Education Act 1902.* Liberal Publication Department

Great Britain (1944) *Education Act 1944 7 and 8 Geo. 6*, Ch.31 London: HMSO

Great Britain (2000) *The Care Standards Act 2000.* London: HMSO

Green, P. (1991) The History and Development of CPVE. In Chitty, C. (ed) *Post-16 Education.* London: Kogan Page Ltd.

Grenfell, M. and James D. (1998) Theory, Practice and Pedagogic Research. In *Bourdieu and Education Acts of Practical Theory.* London: Falmer Press

Griffiths M. (1998) *Educational Research for Social Justice getting off the fence.* Buckingham: Open University Press

Griffiths, M. (2003) *Action Research for Social Justice in Education Fairly Different.* Buckingham: Open University Press

Hargreaves, A. (1989) *Curriculum and Assessment Reform.* Milton Keynes: Open University Press

Hayward G. *et al* (2006) *The Nuffield Review of 14-19 Education and Training Annual Report 2005-2006.* Oxford: University of Oxford

Helsby, G.; Knight, P. and Saunders M. (1998) Preparing Students for the New Work Order: the case of Advanced General National Vocational Qualifications. *British Educational Research Journal* 24 (1) p63-78

Higham, J. and Yeomans, D. (2006) *Emerging provision and practice in 14-19 education and training. A report on the evaluation of the third year of the 14-19 pathfinder initiative.* DfES Research Report RR737 Nottingham: DfES

Hodgson, A and Spours, K. (2003) A Baccalaureate System for the English Context. In G. Phillips and T. Pound (eds) *Baccalaureate.* London: Kogan Page

Hodgson, Ann and Spours, Ken (2007) Specialised diplomas: transforming the 14-19 landscape in England? In *Journal of Education Policy* 22 (6) p657 – 673

Hodkinson P. and Bloomer M. (2000) Learning Careers: continuity and change in young people's dispositions to learning in: *British Educational Research Journal* 26 (5) p583-597

Hodkinson, P. (1996) Careership: The Individual, Choices and Markets in the Transition to Work. In Avis, J. *et al, Knowledge and Nationhood Education, Politics and Work.* London: Cassell

Hodkinson, P. (1998) Career Decision Making and the Transition from School to Work. In M. Grenfell and D. James (eds) *Bourdieu and Education Acts of Practical Theory.* London: Falmer Press

Hodkinson, P. Sparkes, A. and Hodkinson, H. (1996) *Triumphs and Tears: Young People, Markets and the Transition from School to Work.* London: David Fulton

Hoelscher, Michael and Hayward, Geoff (2008) *Degrees of Success – Working Paper 3: Analysing access to HE for students with different educational backgrounds: preliminary descriptive results* [online] available at: http://www.tlrp.org/project%20sites/degrees/documents/Working_Paper_3_MH_GH_final2.doc Accessed 23/08/2008

Holland, M. *et al* (2003) *Pathways to Opportunities and Excellence: Collaborative Curriculum Development at 13+ in South Yorkshire.* Paper presented to the Annual Conference of the British Educational Research Association, Heriot Watt University, Edinburgh, 11-13 September 2003

Holy Bible New Revised Standard Version (1989) Oxford: Oxford University Press/Catholic Truth Society

Hume, David (1740/2000) *A Treatise of Human Nature* (eds David Fate Norton and Mary J. Norton). Oxford: Oxford University Press

Hutton, W. (1995) *The State We're In.* London: Cape

Hyland, Terry (2006) Vocational education and training and the therapeutic turn in *Educational Studies* 32 (3) p299-306

John Paul II (undated) *Catechism of the Catholic Church.* London: Geoffrey Chapman and Vatican City: Libreria Editrice Vaticana

Kant, Immanual (1785/2002) *Groundwork for the Metaphysics of Morals.* New Haven: Yale University Press

Kant, Immanual (2006) *Toward Perpetual Peace and Other Writings on Politics, Peace, and History.* New Haven: Yale University Press

Kristjansson, K. (2007) Justified Self esteem in *Journal of Philosophy of Education* volume. 41 (2) p247-262

Lee, D. (1955/1987) *Plato The Republic.* London: Penguin Books

Lingard, Bob (2005) Socially Just Pedagogies in Changing Times in *International Studies in the Sociology of Education* 15 (2) p165-186

Learning and Skills Council (2007) *Benchmarking data* [online] available at: http://www.lsc. gov.uk/providers/Data/statistics/sfr/ retrieved 20.12.2008

LSC Nottinghamshire (December 2004) *Consultation Draft Strategic Area Review of Foundation/Entry and Level 1 Provision for Post 16 Learners in Nottingham and Nottinghamshire.* Nottinghamshire: Learning and Skills Council

MacIntyre, A. (1981) *After Virtue: A Moral Theory.* London: Duckworth

Macrae, S., Maguire, M. and Ball, S. J. (1997) Whose 'Learning' Society? A Tentative Deconstruction in *Journal of Education Policy* 12 (6) p499-509

Major, B. (1990) The Changing Further Education Structure: A Basis for Conscription? In J. Corbett (ed) *Uneasy Transitions: Disaffection in Post-compulsory Education and Training.* Basingstoke: The Falmer Press

McCulloch, G. (1987) History and Policy: The Politics of TVEI. In D. Gleeson (ed) *TVEI and Secondary Education: a critical appraisal.* Milton Keynes: Open University Press

McCulloch, G. (1991) *Philosophers and Kings Education for Leadership in Modern England.* Cambridge: Cambridge University Press

McCulloch, G. (1994) *Educational Reconstruction: The 1944 Education Act and the Twenty First Century.* London: Routledge

McCulloch, G. (1995) Parity of Esteem and Tripartism in E. Jenkins (ed) *Studies in the History of Education.* Leeds: Leeds University Press

McCulloch, G (1998) *Failing the Ordinary Child? The Theory and Practice of Working Class Secondary Education.* Buckingham: Open University Press

Millman, V. and Weiner, G. (1987) Engendering Equal Opportunities: The Case of TVEI. In D. Gleeson (ed) *TVEI and Secondary Education: a critical appraisal.* Milton Keynes: Open University Press

Minogue, K. (1998) Social Justice in Theory and Practice. In D. Boucher and P. Kelly (eds) *Social Justice from Hume to Walzer.* London:Routledge

Moore, R. (1984) Schooling and the World of Work. In I. Bates *et al, Schooling for the Dole.* Basingstoke: Macmillan Publishers Ltd.

Nuffield Review of 14-19 Education and Training, England and Wales (2007) *Issues Paper 1The New 14-19 Diplomas November 2007* [online] available at: http://www.nuffield14-19review.org.uk/ cgi/ documents/documents.cgi?a=168&t=template.htm accessed 26.09.2008

Objective One South Yorkshire (undated) *Single Programming Document Volume One*. Sheffield: Objective One

Office for National Statistics *Neighbourhood Statistics* available at www.neighbourhood.statistics. gov.uk accessed 25.10.2004; 13.08.2006

OFSTED (2003) *Developing New Vocational Pathways Interim Report on the Introduction of New GCSEs*. E-Publication HMI 1630

OfSTED (1993) *Standards and Quality in Education 1992/93: The annual report of Her Majesty's Chief Inspector of Schools*. London: HMSO

Oxford English Dictionary 2nd Edition (2003) Editor C. Soanes. Oxford: Oxford University Press

Preston J. and Hammond, C. (2003) Practitioner Views on the Wider Benefits of Further Education in *Journal of Further and Higher Education* 27 (2) p211 -222

Pring, R. (1995) *Closing The Gap Liberal Education and Vocational Preparation*. London: Hodder and Stoughton

Qualifications and Curriculum Authority (2008) *Level Descriptors* [online] available at: http://www. qca.org.uk/libraryAssets/media/qca_05_2242_level_descriptors.pdf Accessed 28.10.2008

Raggatt, P. and Williams, S. (1999) *Government, Markets and Vocational Qualifications An Anatomy of Policy*. London: Falmer Press

Rawls, J. (1999) *A Theory of Justice Revised Edition*. Oxford: Oxford University Press

Reay, D. (1995) Using habitus to look at Race and Class in Primary Classrooms. In Morwenna Griffiths and Barry Troyna (eds) *Antiracism, Culture and Social Justice in Education*. Stoke on Trent Trentham Books

Reay, D. (1998) Cultural Reproduction: Mothers Involvement in Their Children's Primary Schooling. In Grenfell, M. and James D. *Bourdieu and Education Acts of Practical Theory*. London: Falmer Press

Reay, D. (2004) It's all becoming a habitus: beyond the habitual use of habitus in educational research in *British Journal of Sociology of Education* 25 (4) p431-443

Reay, D. and Wiliam, D. (1999) I'll be a Nothing Structure, Agency and the Construction of Identity Through Assessment in *British Education Research Journal* 25 (3) p343-55

Riseborough, G. (1993) Learning a Living or Living a Learning? In I. Bates and G. Riseborough (eds) *Youth and Inequality*. Buckingham: Open University Press

Robbins, D. (1998) The Need for an Epistemological 'Break'. In Grenfell, M. and James D. *Bourdieu and Education Acts of Practical Theory*. London: Falmer Press

Robinson, (1997) *The Myth of Parity of Esteem: Earnings and Qualifications* Discussion Paper no 354. London: Centre for Economic Performance

Rogers, Carl (1983) *Freedom to Learn for the 80s*. London: Merrill

Rogers, Carl (1961) *On becoming a person: a therapist's view of psychotherapy*. London: Constable and Co.

Seager, Ashley (2009) School Leaving age may rise to 18 in effort to tackle unemployment The Guardian: *The Guardian*

Sikes, P. and Taylor, M. (1987) Some Problems with Defining, Interpreting and Communicating Vocational Education. In D. Gleeson (ed) *TVEI and Secondary Education: A Critical Appraisal*. Milton Keynes: Open University Press

Skeggs, Bev (1997) *Formations of Class and Gender*. London: Sage

Slee, R. (1997) Disruptive behaviour and the educational wasteland. In S. Tomlinson (ed) *Education 14-19: Critical Perspectives*. London: Athlone Press

Taunton Commission (1868) *Schools Enquiry Commission*. London: HMSO

Tarrant J. (2001) The Ethics of Post-compulsory Education and Training in a Democracy in *Journal of Further and Higher Education* 25 (3) p369-378

Times Education Supplement (2006) report *All They Want Is Fame*. 23 June 2006

Tomlinson, S. (1997). Education 14-19: Divided and Divisive. In S. Tomlinson (ed) *Education 14-19: Critical Perspectives*. London: Athlone Press

Tomlinson, S. (2001) Education Policy 1997-2000: The Effects on Top, Bottom and Middle England in *International Studies in the Sociology of Education* 11 (3) p261-278

Tomlinson, Sally (2005) *Education in a post-welfare society*. Maidenhead: Open University Press

Unwin, L. (1990) The Competence race: We are all qualified now. In J. Corbett (ed) *Uneasy Transitions: Disaffection in Post-compulsory Education and Training*. Basingstoke: The Falmer Press

Unwin, L. and Wellington, J. (2001) *14+ Young People's Perspectives on Education, Training and Employment*. London: Kogan Page

Usher R. and Edwards R. (1994) *Post-Modernism and Education*. London: Routledge

Wallace, S. (2001) Guardian angels and teachers from hell: using metaphor as a measure of schools' experiences and expectations of General National Vocational *Qualifications in Qualitative Studies in Education* 14 (6) p727-739

Wallace, Susan (2008 ed) *Oxford Dictionary of Education*. Oxford: Oxford University Press

Webb, J.; Schirato, T. and Danaher, G. (2002) *Understanding Bourdieu*. Crows Nest NSW: Allen and Unwin

Whitehead, A. N. (1929) *The Aims of Education and Other Essays*. London: Ernest Benn Ltd.

Willis, Paul E. (1978) *Learning to Labour: How Working Class Kids Get Working Class Jobs*. London: Saxon House

Wolf, A. (2002) Qualifications and Assessment. In R. Aldrich (ed.) *A Century of Education*. London: Routledge/Falmer

Woodward, W. (2002) *Learning to Beat the Class System* ONLINE EducationGuardian.co.uk/schools/learning to beat the class system. Reproduced article originally published 02 January 2002 in Guardian Education. Accessed on 11 May 2002

Woolcock, N. (2008, November 14) Good GCSEs but coasting schools must try harder, *The Times: The Times*

Working Group on 14-19 reform (2004b) 14-19 Curriculum and Qualifications Reform Final Report of the Working Group on 14-19 Reform. London: DfES

Working Group on 14-19 Reform (February 2004a) *14-19 Curriculum and Qualifications Reform Interim Report of the Working Group on 14-19 Reform*. London: DfES

Working Group on 14-19 Reform (July 2003) *Principles for Reform of 14-19 Learning Programmes and Qualifications*. London: DfES

Zournazi, M. (2002) Hope, Passion, Politics. Interview with Chantal Mouffe and Ernesto Laclau in *Soundings Issue* 22 p70-85

Index

169